starting out:
attacking play

JAMES PLASKETT

EVERYMAN CHESS

Gloucester Publishers plc   www.everymanchess.com

First published in 2004 by Gloucester Publishers plc (formerly Everyman Publishers plc), Northburgh House, 10 Northburgh Street, London EC1V 0AT

British Library Cataloguing-in-Publication Data
A catalogue record for this book is available from the British Library.

ISBN 1 85744 367 5

Distributed in North America by The Globe Pequot Press, P.O Box 480, 246 Goose Lane, Guilford, CT 06437-0480.

All other sales enquiries should be directed to Everyman Chess, Northburgh House, 10 Northburgh Street, London EC1V 0AT
tel: 020 7253 7887; fax: 020 7490 3708
email: info@everymanchess.com
website: www.everymanchess.com

Everyman is the registered trade mark of Random House Inc. and is used in this work under license from Random House Inc.

EVERYMAN CHESS SERIES (formerly Cadogan Chess)
Chief Advisor: Garry Kasparov
Commissioning editor: Byron Jacobs

Typeset and edited by First Rank Publishing, Brighton.
Cover design by Horatio Monteverde.
Production by Navigator Guides.
Printed and bound in Great Britain by Biddles Ltd.

Contents

Introduction

Attacking Play

Chessplayers love to attack. Whether you are a complete beginner, a club player, a tournament professional or a world champion, there is nothing quite so exciting as organising your forces for a direct assault on the enemy king.

However, adopting an attacking pose does not guarantee success. Strong players have good defensive technique. So, if your attacking play is to succeed, it must be based on sound principles. It is the aim of this book to identify such principles and to show how and why attacking plans can be successful.

To illustrate themes in attack (and, of course to some degree, in defence) I have chosen to concentrate exclusively on my own experiences at the chessboard. I tried, in many of my games, and especially when I had the white pieces, to launch attacks on the enemy king. This policy has been based on the idea that, if I have strengths in chess, they lie more with tactics than with strategy or technique.

Attacking situations are, naturally, often very sharp. Thus the likelihood of the opponent making tactical errors increases in these volatile situations, even if the attack is not 100% correct. When attacking, the chessplayer transforms from the mere competitor into something of the artist, the entertainer, the matador and the magician. Like most people, I guess it was the attacking flair, of the Alekhines, Tals, Spasskys and Fischers – and also their 'Greatest Hits' collections – which first caught my imagination.

Creative Play

When the ELO system was first introduced (circa 1970) World Champion Boris Spassky observed that it was a good measure of a player's results but not a good measure of his creativity. The highest world ranking I ever achieved was 100th, my highest national ranking 7th, my greatest tournament victory was in the 1990 British Championship and the best ELO rating I ever managed was 2529, at the age of 40 in 2000.

But the creative side of the game is harder to quantify, and it was always that which interested me more than the game's technical, grinding, defensive and *Sitzfleisch* aspects. Travelling thousands of miles to trot out a known sequence of opening moves in order to equalise with Black was never really part of my agenda.

In Richard Bach's book, *One*, he describes an ideas foundry where ideas emerge, molten, from the forge to be handled and tendered by artisans. Might we truly access some such place whenever we fashion any new concept?

Attacking Moves

'Shah Mat!' The King is dead. Shah itself, like Tzar and Kaiser, is a corruption of the name of Caesar, and testament to his achievements. And so the Persian cry itself became 'Checkmate! The King is dead.' Any move which aims to favourably alter the balance of a position, be it in the form of a weakening of the opponent's structure, a disruption of his co-ordination or a misplacing of one of his pieces is (of course) in essence an attacking move. This can be any move that is in the proper spirit of trying for more than merely avoiding defeat – it need not, to satisfy the proper criteria, directly threaten the enemy king. In these pages, however, only those games in which the pieces' blood is spilled shall be considered as true acts of aggression on the chess board.

James Plaskett,
Playa Flamenca,
Spain,
October 2004

Chapter One

Rook's Pawn Tin Openers

'Pawns can be legitimate attacking pieces' is what Kasparov once told me. How to 'storm the enemy barricades' or break into a secure haven is very often the attacker's problem. To effect a breach we will often see him throw pawns at the opponent's king position, but the use of a rook's pawn to carve a way in is different to a pawn storm *per se*. In its most recognised form, the defender will have advanced a knight's pawn one square, after which the attacker's rook's pawn reaches the fifth rank and then executes the trade, thus opening up a route for an incursion of major pieces. Very often the advance of the opponent's knight's pawn is part of a fianchetto set-up of the defending bishop, which the attacker will attempt to eliminate with his own bishop in order to weaken the defences. Indeed this bishop is so important a piece to the defender that it is occasionally kept in play by sacrificing a rook for the attacker's bishop rather than acquiescing to the exchange.

Frequently the most effective response to a flank attack is a counter-reaction in the centre.

This is a scenario which often crops up in such fianchetto systems as the Sicilian Dragon, the Samisch Kings Indian and the Pirc Defence. But if the knight's pawn in front of the defending king is unmoved, then the advancing rook's pawn might not be able to open up a file. Instead it can serve a vital attacking function in denting the foundations of the king's castle, as well as forming a crampon to facilitate future infiltration.

Game 1
☐ **Plaskett** ■ **Murshed**
Dhaka 1998

1 e4 d6 2 d4 Nf6

There are those who would say this is inexact due to the set-ups involving Be3.

3 Nc3 g6 4 Be3 Bg7

There are also some players who believe this, too, is inaccurate, recommending instead deferring development of the bishop with something like 4...c6 5 f3 Qb6!?, as in Haygarth–Mestel, British Championship 1974, Clacton, or 5...b5 with emphasis initially on the development of the queenside.

5 Qd2 0-0

And I definitely remember reading somewhere that castling so early in this system offers White an attack on a plate. Perhaps Murshed read different books!? He certainly has shown skill in handling the Pirc Defence, as was demonstrated in W.Watson-Murshed, British Championship 1988, Blackpool: 1 e4 Nf6 2 Nc3 d6 3 d4 g6 4 Nf3 Bg7 5 Bg5 c6 6 Qd2 Bg4 7 Qf4 Bf3 8 Qf3 Qa5 9 h4 h6 10 Bf4 Nbd7 11 0-0-0 e5 12 de5 Ne5 13 Qe2 0-0-0 14 Qd2 Nfd7 15 Kb1 Nc5 16 Be2 b5 17 a3 Nc4 18 Bc4 bc4 19 f3 Rd7 20 Ka2 Rb7 21 Rb1 Rd8 22 Bh6 (**Diagram 1**)

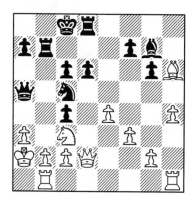

Diagram 1
A powerful bishop

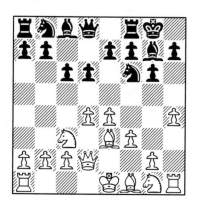

Diagram 2
Opening the tin

22...Rb2! 23 Rb2 Bc3 24 Qc1 Na4 25 Rb1 d5 26 Bf4 Bb2 27 Qe1 c3 28 Bc1 Qc5 29 Rb2 cb2 30 Bb2 Nb2 31 Kb2 Rd7 32 Qd2 de4 33 Qe2 Rb7 34 Ka2 Qb5 White resigned.

6 f3

6 Bh6 can be considered here.

6...c6 7 h4 (Diagram 2)

I appreciated the mechanics of the situation here and promptly got on with the attack. Perhaps this thrust was also strong a move earlier.

7...e5

Apparently this natural move was a theoretical novelty, which is indicative of the rarity of such early castling in this line.

8 Nge2 ed4 9 Nd4 d5 (Diagram 3)

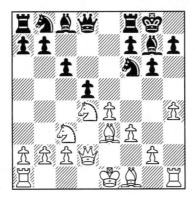
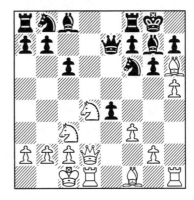

Diagram 3
A central counter

Diagram 4
Charging forwards

10 0-0-0

I was confident that my development lead – together with the attacking superiority that White is supposedly afforded by Black's early castling – would enable me to cope with any tricks in the middle. 10 e5? Nh5 looked quite wrong for White.

10...de4

Black's development disadvantage rules out 10...c5?, when after 11 Nb3 d4 12 Nc5 Nc6 13 Bd4 Ne4 14 N5e4 there is insufficient compensation for the pawn.

11 Bh6!?

This is the way to play such a formation, and here there is the threat of 12 Bg7 Kg7 13 Ne6 Be6 14 Qd8 Rd8 15 Rd8 with a killing pin.

11...Qe7 12 h5!? (Diagram 4)

Careering merrily on. My attitude and moves in this game have much to do with the influence of Shirov. Whether Alexei himself wishes to be associated with it, I do not know.

12...c5?

A decisive error. 12...ef3 13 hg6 fg6 14 Bc4 Kh8 15 gf3 grant White some attacking compensation, as do 12...e3 13 Be3 Nh5 14 Bh6 and 13... Nh5 14 Ne4. After the text, however, there is a forced win because many of my pieces hit almost optimum attacking posts.

13 hg6! fg6

There is nothing better. In the event of 13...hg6 14 Bg7 e3 15 Qe1! Kg7 16 Qh4 the attack triumphs down the h-file. 13...cd4 14 gh7 Nh7 15 Bg7 e3 16 Qd3 wins for White, as does 14...Kh8 15 Bg7 Kg7 16 h8Q! Rh8 17 Qg5. The interference move 13...e3 is the hardest to handle. **(Diagram 5)**

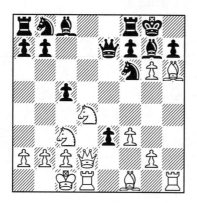

Diagram 5
Interference

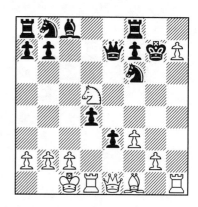

Diagram 6
A deflection

White should respond with 14 gh7 Kh8 (or 14...Nh7 15 Qd3) 15 Bg7 Kg7 16 Qe1! cd4 (16...Rh8 17 Qh4 wins, while after 16...Kh8 it would be, at last, time for White to just tuck away his attacked knight with 17 Nb3) 17 Nd5! **(Diagram 6)**

It is important to keep feeding more pieces into the attack and/or strip away defensive pieces. Now 17...Nd5 loses to 18 h8Q! Rh8 19 Qg3 Kf6 20 Rh8 when the black king is exposed and the attack still rages on. 17...Qe5 meets with 18 Qh4! when Black has nothing better than 18...Nh5 19 Qh5 Qh5 20 Rh5 Nc6 21 Bb5 and his centre pawns will fall. Note 18...Kh8 here serves only to weather the first wave since after 19 Nf6 the defences will not hold much longer.

14 Bc4 Kh8 (Diagram 7)

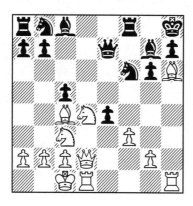

Diagram 7
White spots a switchback

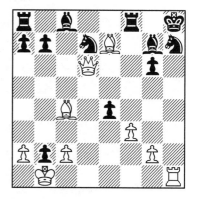

Diagram 8
A White success

15 Bg5!

An unexpected but highly effective switchback.

15...cd4

In the case of 15...e3 16 Qe1 the threat of a rook sacrifice on h7 looms (as in the game), and 15...h5 is a chronic weakening that runs into the standard response of 16 g4!, when Black cannot survive, e.g. 16...cd4 17 gh5 Be6 18 Nd5! and White comes crashing through.

16 Rh7!

Murshed's body language indicated that he had not foreseen this move. I am unsure what he had been expecting.

16...Nh7

16...Kh7 17 Rh1 Bh6 18 Bh6 is devastating (but not 18 Bf6? which invites the impolite 18...e3!), e.g. 18...Nh5 19 Bf8 (threatening mate on h6) 19...Qf8 20 Ne4 and White – only one piece behind – has strong threats (21 g4) and a vicious attack.

17 Be7 dc3 18 Qd6

Materially Black is not doing at all badly, but his king's safety has been blown to smithereens and defeat is inevitable.

18...cb2 19 Kb1 Nd7 20 Rh1 1-0 (Diagram 8)

Game 2
□ **Iskov** ■ **Plaskett**
Regency Masters, Ramsgate 1979

1 g3 f5 2 b3 e5 3 d4 ed4 4 Qd4

A new position for theory. The early queen development is certainly not out of the question but, on this occasion, it did not work out well.

4...Nf6!? (Diagram 9)

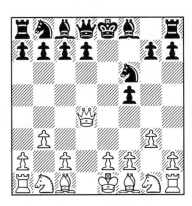

Diagram 9
A Gambit!

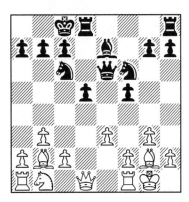

Diagram 10
Time for the tin opener

I doubted that Iskov would accept the gambit pawn with 5 Qe5 Be7 6 Qf5 as Black clearly generates considerable activity. 4...Nc6, incidentally, is a perfectly healthy move, too.

5 Bb2 Be7 6 Bg2 d5 7 Nh3 Nc6 8 Qd1 Be6! 9 Nf4 Qd7

A correct scheme of development as castling long fits in well here. Preserving the prelate with 9...Bf7 is a good alternative.

10 Ne6 Qe6 11 0-0 0-0-0

Black has more space and well placed pieces. Since White has so few active possibilities his game may already be beyond saving.

12 e3 (Diagram 10)

12 Nd2 is probably better, although Black still has a fine game. Now it's time for the tin opener...

12...h5! 13 Nd2

13 h4 prevents the advance but constitutes a grave weakening, and I might have followed up with 13...Rdg8 or even the immediate 13...Ne4!?, perhaps.

13...h4 14 Nf3 hg3 15 hg3 Ne4

An aggressor in itself, while the knight advance also clears the path for the queen to come to the h-file. White is lost.

16 Qe2 Rh5 17 Ne5 Rdh8 18 Nc6 (Diagram 11)

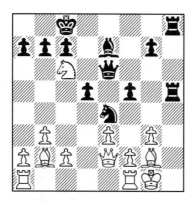

Diagram 11
No need to recapture

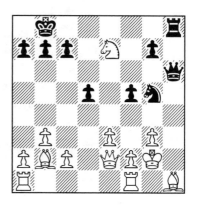

Diagram 12
Highly effective

18...Rh1! 19 Bh1 Qh6

There's no escape for White.

20 Ne7 Kb8 21 Kg2 Ng5 0-1 (Diagram 12)

Black closes the door.

A dramatic example of the tin opener at its most simple and effective.

Next we see a defensive structure unaltered by the tin opener, which instead slips by to help create mating threats.

Game 3

□ **Anand** ■ **Plaskett**

British Championship, Blackpool 1988

1 e4 c5 2 Nf3 e6 3 d4 cd4 4 Nd4 Nc6 5 Nc3 Qc7 6 Be3 a6 7 Qd2!? Nf6 8 f3

At the time of the game this system against the Taimanov was not so well known.

8...b5 (Diagram 13)

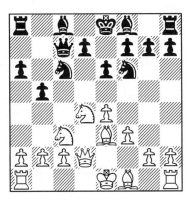

Diagram 13
The Taimanov variation

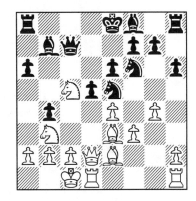

Diagram 14
The English Attack

9 0-0-0

At the 1998 *Monarch Assurance Open* in the Isle of Man, Jaan Ehlvest played 9 g4 against me here. Prompted by my opening's success versus Anand, I continued in a similar vein: 9...h6 10 0-0-0 b4!? 11 Na4 Ne5!? 12 Be2 Bb7 13 Nb3 d5. Once again Black was able to make this liberating move in one go and not – as is so often the case in lines of the English Attack versus the Najdorf or Scheveningen – after the initial d7...d6. There followed 14 Nac5 (**Diagram 14**) 14...Nc4!? (perhaps not best, but intriguing) 15 Bc4 dc4 16 Qb4 cb3 17 Qb7 Qb7 18 Nb7 ba2 19 Kd2 Nd7 (**Diagram 15**)

Here the computers find 20 Bd4!, but neither of us could and instead the game continued 20 Ke2?! Rb8 21 Nd6 Bd6 22 Rd6 Rb2 23 Ra6 0-0 24 Rd1 Ne5. This ought probably to be tenable for White but the odd pawn on a2 must have thrown him, and he fell down a tactical hole, 25 Rd2 Nc4 26 Bd4 Rd8 27 Ra4 e5 prompting his resignation.

9...b4!? 10 Na4 Ne5!?

In uncharted territory I came up with an interesting plan. It's not out of the question that if White falls asleep Black may even go after the knight on a4 with his bishop.

11 Nb3 Rb8

Aimed simply at covering b6.

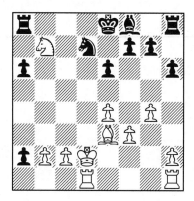

Diagram 15
Spot the computer move

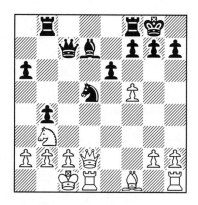

Diagram 16
Black stands well

12 Bc5

This unusual idea did not impress me. Phil Harris preferred 12 Qf2.

12...Bc5 13 Nac5 d5!

Activity.

14 ed5

12 f4? Nc4 is good for Black.

14...Nd5 15 f4 Nd7

Not 13...Nf4?? 14 Qf4 Nd3 15 Nd3 when all is covered.

16 Nd7

Anand, one of the great attackers himself, was naturally loathe to grant me an attack down a newly opened a-file by ever taking on a6. In doing so he would have opened the tin – or can of worms – himself.

16...Bd7

The d5-knight is now excellently centralised.

17 f5 0-0 (Diagram 16)

Black emerges from his opening experiment with rather more than mere equality. He has a development edge and attacking chances.

18 Be2 Rfd8

Lining up against the enemy queen.

19 Bf3 (Diagram 17)

19...Ba4!

Beginning a sharp attacking sequence which leads to my advantage.

20 fe6 Bb3! 21 ef7 Kf8 22 ab3 Nc3! (Diagram 18) 23 Qd8

White tries to bail out into an ending with a rook and bishop for the queen, hoping to be able to hold out by erecting an unassailable fortress. But this is not quite possible because Black has a tin opener up his sleeve.

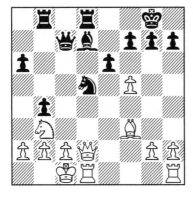

Diagram 17
Black has a sharp attack

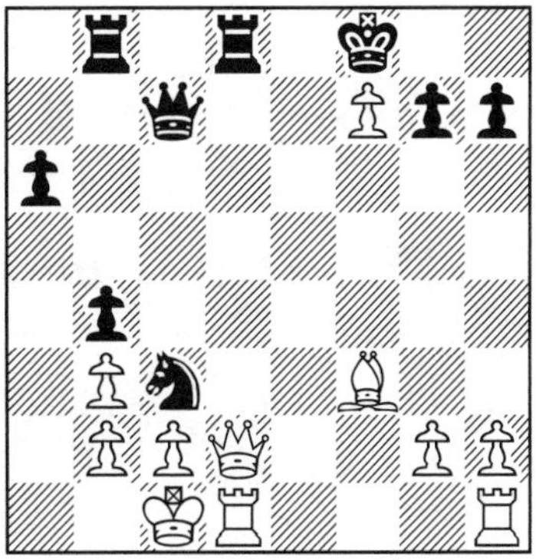

Diagram 18
White tries to bail out

23...Rd8 24 bc3 bc3 25 Kb1 Rd1

25...Rd2!? is interesting.

26 Rd1 Qa5 (Diagram 19)

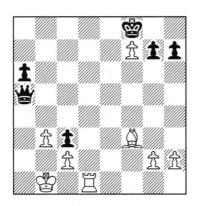

Diagram 19
Can Black be kept at bay?

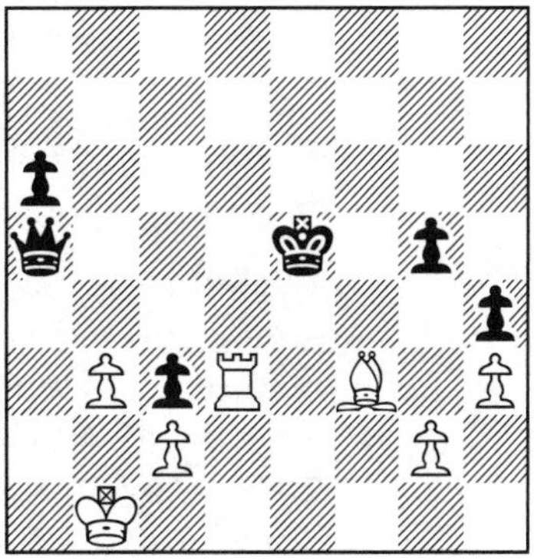

Diagram 20
Activating the king

27 Rd3

Forced in view of the threatened 25...Qa3 with mate to follow.

27...Kf7

Finally eliminating the pawn.

28 h3 Kf6 29 Ba8 h5 30 Bf3 g6 31 Ba8 g5 32 Bf3 h4 33 Ba8 Ke6 34 Bf3 Ke5 (Diagram 20) 35 Ba8

The pawn ending after 35 Rd5 is lost: 35...Qd5 36 Bd5 Kd5 37 Kc1 Ke4 38 Kd1 Ke3 39 Ke1 a5 with zugzwang, after which White must permit the black king entry. So Vishy continues to oscillate and to challenge Black to actually demonstrate something.

35...Qc5 36 Bf3 Qa5 37 Ba8 Qb4 38 Ka2 Qa5 39 Kb1 Qc5 40 Ka2 Ke6 41 Bf3 a5! After some fiddling around Black gets on with the correct technical procedure. In this particular instance this is to dismantle a fortress by attack, the critical weapon being the tin opener!

42 Bh5 a4 (Diagram 21)

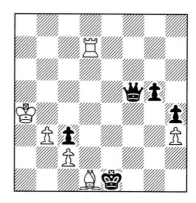

Diagram 21	**Diagram 22**
Black infiltrates	Success

43 Bg4 Ke5 44 Bf3 Kf4 45 Bd5

Of course capturing the pawn is out of the question due to 45...Qb4.

45...a3!

An unexpected role for the tin opener! Black aims to mix various themes, for example the advance of the a-pawn, mating threats, penetration of by the king into enemy territory camp and the possible sacrifice of the queen to create a far advanced passed c-pawn. White cannot cope with all of these problems. 46 Kb1 meets with 46...Qg1 47 Ka2 Qc1, while 46 Bb7 Qg1 is final, e.g. 47 Rc3 Qc1 or 47 Ka3 Qa7. 'L.P.D.O... loose pieces drop off', as Dr John Nunn accurately observes. 46 Ba8 Qg1 47 Ka3 Qa1 48 Kb4 Qa8 and there will be no adequate fortress, e.g. 49 Rf3 Qf3 50 gf3 Kf3 and the h-pawn queens, or 49 Rd4 Kf5 50 Rg4 Qa1 51 Rd4 Qe1 52 Rd3 Qd2 etc.

46 Bf3

So the sentinel must let the enemy king infiltrate...

46...Kg3

Deep...

47 Ba8 Kf2

...inside the walls of the citadel.

48 Bf3 Qf5!

Threatening to take the rook. Now 49 Rc3 loses to 49...Qe5 and the attacked rook is 'pinned' thanks to the mate on b2, while 49 Ka3 even invites mate with 49...Qa5 etc.

49 Bd1 Ke1

And again!

50 Rd8 Qf6 51 Rd5 Qf2

The fortress collapses.

52 Rd3 Qg2 53 Ka3 Qe4

Renewing the threat to capture the rook.

54 Rd7 Qa8 55 Kb4 Qf8 56 Ka4

56 Kc3 Qc8.

56...Qf5 0-1 (Diagram 22)

White resigned because 57 Bg4 Qc2 58 Rc7 Qe4 59 Kc3 Qe5 spells the end.

Game 4
□ **Plaskett** ■ **Larsen**
London GLC 1986

---

1 e4 c5 2 Nf3 Nc6 3 Bb5 Qb6

Miles played this with success in the 1970s (against Sax and Torre, for example).

4 Bc6!? Qc6

Miles once recaptured with the b-pawn.

5 0-0!? (Diagram 23)

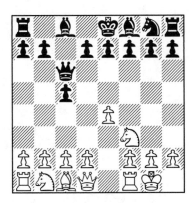
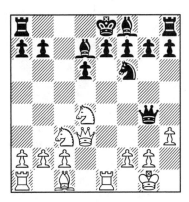

Diagram 23
A natural gambit

Diagram 24
Unnecessary

A natural enough gambit. I first noticed it in the game Short-Fuller back in 1976.

5...d6

5...Qe4 6 Nc3 with compensation.

6 d4 cd4

6...Qe4 7 Nc3 again leaves White with play for the pawn, but 6 ...Bg4!? deserves attention.

7 Nd4 Qe4

Larsen rarely ducked a challenge.

8 Nc3 Qg4 9 Qd3

New territory, but I was confident that I had a pawn's worth of play.

9...Bd7 10 Re1 Nf6 11 h3? (Diagram 24)

11 Ndb5! is a much better move.

11...Qg6! 12 Qf3 Rb8

Addressing the threat to b7, but I think the more natural 12...0-0-0 is stronger.

13 Ndb5

This is practically forced. After the inaccuracy at move eleven White must be content with a middlegame in which in return for the pawn there are attacking chances thanks to Black's development problems.

13...e5 (Diagram 25)

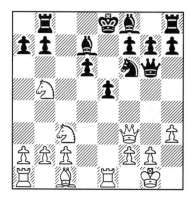 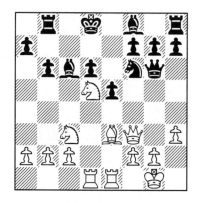

Diagram 25
White can dislodge the black king

Diagram 26
A central grip

13...Bc6? is refuted by 14 Nd6 Kd7 15 Nde4, e.g. 15...Ne4 16 Ne4 f5 17 Qd3 Kc8 18 Ng5 h6 19 Re6 Qh5 20 Qf5 etc. However, 13...e6 might be a better try.

14 Nc7

14 Na7? achieves nothing.

14... Kd8 15 N7d5 Bc6

It makes sense to pin and activate. Throughout the execution of his middlegame initiative White must constantly monitor the g2-square.

16 Be3 b6

This time the threat to capture on a7 with the bishop is a genuine one.

17 Rad1 (Diagram 26)

White is fully mobilised. Black, on the other hand, lags in development, while his king remains stuck in the centre. The price is a pawn.

17...Rc8 18 a4!

Here we have an a-pawn tin opener, the aim being to infiltrate Black's king position.

Following his participation in the 1972 San Antonio event Larsen promised RHM Publishing that he would be writing them a book entitled *Tactical and Strategical use of the Rook's Pawns...* we await its appearance but, if it ever hits the streets, perhaps Bent has a game for it here!?

18...Ba8

Already way behind in development, Black can ill afford to spend more time picking up another pawn on a4 or c2. 18...Bb7 is an important alternative – after 19 a5 Rc3 20 bc3 e4 21 Qe2 Nd5 22 ab6 ab6 23 Qb5 the queen will make an emphatic entrance into the attack.

19 a5!

White wastes no time.

19...b5

In the event of 19...Rc3 20 bc3 e4 21 Qe2 Nd5 22 Qa6 the queen looks deadly.

20 Ba7! b4 21 Nb5! Be7 (Diagram 27)

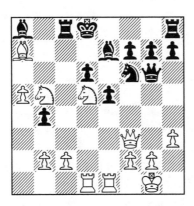

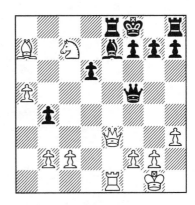

Diagram 27
Black is falling apart

Diagram 28
Black's rook is stuck

Or 21...Nd5 22 Rd5 and White retains a powerful attack even if Black takes the exchange, e.g. 22...Qe6 23 Ree5! Qe5 24 Bb6! Kd7 25 Qf7 Qe7? 26 Rd6 mate.

22 Re5!

White introduces another piece into the attack, in the process removing a valuable chunk of the defensive wall.

22...Nd5

22...de5 23 Nf6 is final.

23 Red5 Ke8

Black runs, but it is too late.

24 Re1

White remains focused.

24...Kf8 25 Qe3! Re8

25...Bf6 26 Nd6 with the threaten of mate on e8.

26 Nc7! Bd5 27 Nd5 Qf5

In reply to 27...Qg5 White can maintain the pressure with 28 Qd4 when his attack has less bite but his development lead and monster a-pawn are no less significant. With the text Black now hopes for 28 Ne7 Qd7.

28 Nc7! (Diagram 28)

The rook cannot sidestep the attack.

28...Qe5 29 Qe5 de5 30 Ne8 Ke8 31 Re5

Now White needs only to tidy up in order to secure the full point.

31...Kd7 32 Be3 Bd6 33 Rd5 Ke6 34 Rd2 Ra8 35 Bb6 Be5 36 b3 f5 37 Kf1 g5 38 Ke2 Bc3 39 Rd8 1-0

Black lost on time.

Game 5
□ **Plaskett** ■ **Clarke**
British Championship 1978, Ayr

1 e4 e6 2 d4 d5 3 Nd2 de4 4 Ne4 Nd7

I had some other attacking adventures in Rubinstein French waters. In the 1978 European Junior Championship, Hungarian Tibor Karolyi played 4...Bd7!?, which became popularised as 'The Fort Knox' variation. After 5 Nf3 Bc6 6 Bd3 Nd7 I continued 7 0-0. FM Graham Lee always plays the Rubinstein with Black, even venturing it against me in an earlier round of the 1978 British. He observes that those who play 3 Nc3 tend to castle queenside, whereas those who play 3 Nd2 castle short. This game went 7...Ngf6 8 Qe2 Be7 9 Nf6 Bf6 10 Rd1 Qe7 11 Bf4 0-0-0 12 Bb5 Bf3 (12...Bb5 is wiser) 13 Qf3 a6 14 Bf1 Rhe8 (**Diagram 29**)

A fundamental dilemma when deciding how to take on a castled king (an area that is not often addressed in texts on attack) is whether to attack with pawns (15 b4!?) or with pieces (15 Rd3!?). White might also consider not attacking, since 15 c3 leaves him with the bishop pair. I chose 15 Rd3!?, when there followed 15...e5 16 Rb3 e4 (16...c6? 17 Ba6) 17 Qc3 Nb8 18 Be2!? (intending a killer check on g4 and hence a very unusual way of inducing weaknesses in the opponent's camp) 18...b5 (definitely not the sort of concession we want to make) 19 Qh3 Kb7 20 a4 (aiming at Black's vulnerable bits) 20...b4 21 c3 Nc6 22 Bc4 (22 Qf5 is also strong as White then threatens to take on a6) 22...Bd4 (desperation – the king's roof is about to cave in) 23 cd4 Na5 24 Rc1 g5 25 Bd2 c5 26 dc5! Rd2 27 Rb4 Ka8 28 Ba6 and Black's cause was now quite hopeless, White winning on the 37th move.

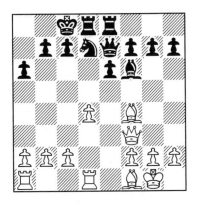

Diagram 29
Attack with pawns or pieces?

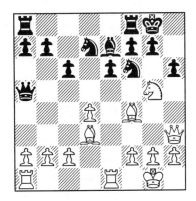

Diagram 30
How to continue the attack?

In 1998 I played GM Keith Arkell in Newcastle, and (after 4...Bd7 5 Nf3 Bc6 6 Bd3 Nd7) I varied with 7 Qe2 Ngf6 8 Neg5!? (a provocative continuation with echoes of 1 e4 c6 2 d4 d5 3 Nd2 de4 4 Ne4 Nd7 5 Ng5!?) 8...Bf3 9 Qf3 c6 10 0-0 Be7 11 Re1 Qa5 12 Bf4 0-0? (12...Nf8!? might have been the safest way to avoid an unwelcome sacrifice, albeit dreadfully passive) 13 Qh3 h6 (**Diagram 30**) 14 Ne6! fe6 15 Qe6 Rf7 16 Bc4 Nd5 17 Qd7 Bb4 (this move complicates matters but not enough to deny White the win) 18 Re8 Bf8 19 Qf7! Kf7 20 Ra8 Qb4 21 Bb3 Qd4 22 Be3 Qb2 23 Rd1 Qa5 24 Ra7 Kg6 25 Bd5 cd5 26 Rb7 and White had a trivially won game, although my subsequent technique was so poor that we ended up agreeing a draw on the 63rd move. Nobody called my failure to win from this position 'almost unforgivable' but they could have done.

5 Nf3 Be7

In a league game from 1997, Jonathan Speelman played 5...Ngf6 against me. Play went 6 Bg5 h6 7 Nf6 Nf6 8 Bh4. I had played this in order to try out something against a Speelmanic invention which he had hatched in the second game of his 1988 Candidates Quarter Final match against Short. There followed 8...g6!? 9 Bc4!? (**Diagram 31**)

Diagram 31
A novelty

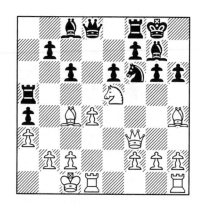

Diagram 32
An unusual rook development

This was my novelty, after which play went 9...Bg7 (9...g5 10 Bg3 g4
11 Nh4 Qd4? 12 Nf5 wins for White) 10 Qe2 0-0 11 0-0-0 c6 12 Ne5
a5!? 13 Qf3! (a nasty pin) 13...a4 14 a3 Ra5 (**Diagram 32**). A cute try
but, very probably, not a good move as the rook finds itself out of the
game. However, there is little in the way of natural alternatives. 15
g4 Qe7 16 Kb1 c5 17 g5 (inflicting some structural damage on Black)
17...Nh5 18 gh6 Qh4 19 hg7 Ng7 20 d5 b5 (20...ed5 21 Bd5 helps only
White) 21 de6! (**Diagram 33)**

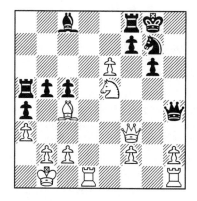

Diagram 33
How does White meet 21...bc4?

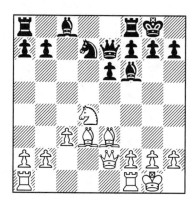

Diagram 34
Can White generate an attack?

Now in reply to 21...bc4 I had ideas of 22 ef7 and 23 Ng6 but, when I
showed this game to GM Vyecheslav Tkachiev, before my hand had
even left c4 he demonstrated 22 Qf7! and White wins. Sharp, these
Russians. Instead the game went 21...Ne6 22 Be6 Be6 23 Rhg1 and
White's attack was beginning to gain pace, with avenues opening to-

ward the black king, which lacks defenders and stands behind a compromised pawn structure. Additionally, the rook on a5 now looks absurd, Black needing to spend time bringing it back into the game. The game developed as follows: 23...Raa8 24 Qd3 (this should have been decisive now that the defences have been breached) 24...c4 25 Rg6! Kh7 26 Rg4 cd3 27 Rh4 Kg7 28 Nd3 and, with two extra pawns, we would expect the battle to be over... Alas, here was another advantage I failed to convert, with another 63rd move draw. This time IM Malcolm Pein did call my failure to win from such a position 'almost unforgivable' and this was fair comment.

6 Bd3 Ngf6 7 Nf6 Bf6 8 Qe2 Qe7 9 0-0 c5 10 Be3

A solid if not too ambitious treatment.

10...0-0 11 c3 cd4 12 Nd4 (Diagram 34) 12...g6 13 Rad1 Bg7 14 Rfe1 Nf6

Clarke regroups ingeniously, but neglects to get his whole team out on the field. White's development lead now starts to count for something.

15 Bf4 a6

Black is concerned about a knight incursion on b5 but he falls further behind.

16 Qf3

A useful way of impeding Black's queenside development.

16...Qc5 17 Nb3

Perhaps this is not a good idea: the horse was already well placed.

17...Qb6 18 Be5

An attacking move that is designed to weaken Black's king by exchanging bishops.

18... Nd7 19 Bg7 Kg7 (Diagram 35)

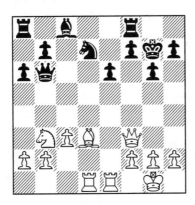

Diagram 35
The dark squares are weak

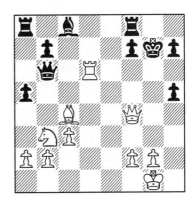

Diagram 36
The king hunt is on

The exchange of dark squared bishops has served to weaken Black's kingside a little, a factor that invites the thematic...

20 h4

The tin opener!

20...a5

The distractor.

21 h5 e5

After 21...a4 22 Nd4 Qb2 White would be so far ahead that he could start to look at sacrifices, e.g. 23 hg6 hg6 24 Bg6! and Black collapses after either 24...fg6 25 Ne6 Kg8 26 Nf8 Nf8 27 Rd8 Qa3 28 Ree8 Qc1 29 Qd1! Qd1 30 Rd1 and 31 Rdd8 or 24...Kg6 25 Qg4 Kf6 26 Ne6! etc.

22 Bc4 Nf6

This time 22...a4 23 Nd2 Qb2?! 24 Ne4 leaves White with splendid activity, while in response to the superior 23...Nf6 White has the effective 24 Qg3.

23 h6!? Kh6 24 Re5

Now, of course, the skewer with ...Bg4 is dodged by 25 Qf4 check.

24...Kg7 25 Qf4

The removal of the dark squared bishops plus White's domination causes Black problems. For example 25...Bf5 here fails to 26 Rf5 gf5 27 Rd6 and 28 Qg5, and after 25...Be6 26 Be6 fe6 27 Nd4 White piles on the pressure against e6.

25...Nh5 26 Rh5

Of course.

26... gh5 27 Rd6 (Diagram 36) 27...Qc7 28 Qf6

I thought the king hunt more fun than 28 Rg6. The rest is simple.

28...Kg8 29 Rd5 Re8 30 Rg5 Kf8 31 Qg7 Ke7 32 Re5 Kd8 33 Qf6 Re7 34 Qh8 Kd7 35 Rd5 Kc6 36 Rc5 Kb6 37 Rc7 Kc7 38 Qf6 Re1 39 Kh2 Bd7 40 Qf4 Kb6 41 Qd6 Bc6 42 Na5! Ra5 43 Qd8 Kc5 44 Qd4 mate.

Game 6
☐ **Plaskett** ■ **J.Anderson**
Lloyds Bank Guernsey Open 1982

---

1 d4 Nf6 2 c4 e6 3 Nf3 b6 4 a3 Be7 5 Nc3 d5 6 cd5 Nd5?! (Diagram 37)

In conjunction with 4...Be7 this is an inaccuracy as White is able to create a formidable pawn centre in one move, which would not have been possible against 4...Bb7. So Black ought to have recaptured with the pawn here.

7 e4 Nc3 8 bc3 0-0 9 Bd3 Bb7 10 0-0 c5 11 Qe2 Nc6 12 Bb2

A recent spate of spectacular Kasparov victories in this formation had made this line popular.

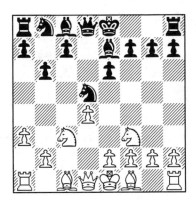

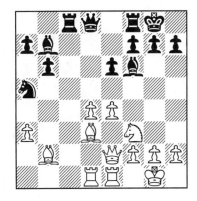

Diagram 37
White gets the centre

Diagram 38
White's position has tremendous energy

12...cd4 13 cd4 Bf6 14 Rad1 Na5

14...Nd4? 15 Bd4 Bd4 is hardly palatable, and after 16 Bc4 Black would be in a bad way. However, the knight is not doing much on a5.

15 Rfe1 Rc8 (Diagram 38)

White's mobilisation is complete. Is there now a way for him to proceed? Or is it a case of being all dressed up with nowhere to go?

16 h4! Rc7?!

There is no immediate refutation of 16...Bh4. White has interesting possibilities such as 17 Ne5, or he might hope to make use of the h-file avenue with 17 g3!?, as I think I had intended, with Kg2 and Rh1 to follow. But in neither instance were matters 100% clear, whereas now the advancing h-pawn is an important addition to the attack.

Stean told me that Seirawan was a great believer in the defensive potential of positions. Keene wrote how Seirawan always impressed him with his confidence in accepting his opponents' gambits. And Yasser himself – who once wrote an article entitled *Gimme your pawns, baby!* – once told me: 'If you're scared, you shouldn't play chess!'

Had Black taken on h4 he would at least have had the booty as compensation.

17 h5 Qc8 18 h6 g6

Well, we have dented the tin.

19 Ne5 Bg5 (Diagram 39)

19...Be5 20 de5 would have left the dark square damage near Black's king all the more apparent. Now it's time to go to work.

20 d5!

Here we go.

20...ed5 21 ed5 Bd5 22 Ng6! hg6 23 Qh5! (Diagram 40)

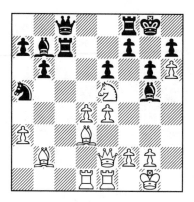

Diagram 39
Time for a central breakthrough

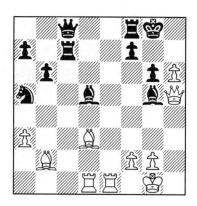

Diagram 40
A neat combination

A known combinational theme, but still the only time I ever pulled it off. 23 Qe5 f6 24 Qd5 Kh7 25 Re6 would also have been powerful.

23...Kh7

23...gh5 24 h7 mate. Now I regain the piece.

24 Qg5 f5 25 Bb5 Bc4 26 Bc4 Nc4 27 Re7 Rf7 28 Rf7 Rf7 29 Rd8 Qd8 30 Qd8 Nb2 31 Qd4 1-0

Game 7
□ **Plaskett** ■ **Chandler**
London GLC 1986

1 Nf3 Nf6 2 d4 e6 3 c4 b6 4 Nc3 Bb7 5 Bg5 Be7 (Diagram 41)

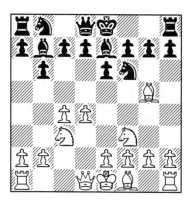

Diagram 41
Solid play

Diagram 42
A useful space advantage

This simple development of the bishop is more solid than 5...Bb4. Note that this game was played in the last round, with Chandler needing only a draw to tie for first place.

6 Qc2 d5

6...c5 has been more common, but the text leads to a sensible form of the Queen's Gambit Declined.

7 cd5 Nd5 8 Be7 Qe7 9 e4 Nc3 10 bc3 0-0 11 Bc4 (Diagram 42)

A Semi-Tarrasch materialises. I had little experience in this opening, and was unsure whether the bishop ought to go to c4 or d3. Then it struck me that my opponent was probably equally unsure.

11...c5 12 0-0 Nc6 13 Rad1 cd4 14 cd4 Rac8 15 Qe2 Na5?!

I don't like this. Just as in the previous game the knight ends up marginalized and away from the action. 15...Rfd8 had to be better.

16 Bd3 Rc3

My a-pawn has not moved so the rook has little to do here.

17 Rfe1 Rd8 (Diagram 43)

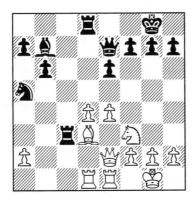

Diagram 43
Is d5 possible?

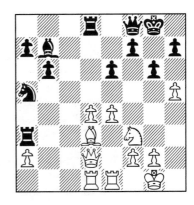

Diagram 44
h6 or hg6?

Mustered behind their pawn centre, White's forces contain a lot of kinetic energy. Michael Stean once remarked of an analogous situation 'I used to think Black was better in those positions until one day someone went d4-d5! against me' and indeed I spent half an hour looking for outlets with d4-d5 ideas. However, I was unconvinced by any of it and, finally, my eye alighted on the h-pawn (odd that it took me so long, given my precedent of the Anderson game). Consequently, having calculated hardly any variations...

18 h4! g6?

After half an hour's thought himself, Black produces his big error. 18...h6 was far more rational. Now, with his self-inflicted weaknesses on the dark squares, Black could already be lost.

19 Qd2 Ra3?!

This whole escapade is misguided; Chandler needed the rook for defence – on a3 it is pretty functionless.

20 h5 Qf8 (Diagram 44) 21 h6

Better than 21 hxg6. Once again the h6-pawn will form the basis of long term attacking possibilities. Were Black now to re-centralise his knight with 21...Nc6, then White's forces would flood in after 22 d5!, e.g. 22...ed5 23 ed5 Rd5 24 Qb2! Rd8 25 Bc4 with terrible threats.

21...Rc8 22 Rc1 f6 23 Rc8 Qc8 24 Rc1 Qd8 25 Qe2 Qf8 26 Qd2 Qd8 27 Rd1 Qd6 (Diagram 45)

Diagram 45
White has a chance

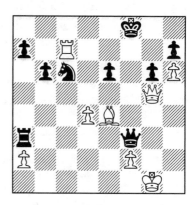

Diagram 46
Overload!

Now I get a clear opportunity to infiltrate, although it is highly implausible that Black can hold. The stranded queenside pieces prove to be a decisive factor.

28 e5! Qf8

Or 28...fe5 29 Ne5 with a vicious attack, e.g. 29...Qd4 30 Bg6 Qd2 31 Rd2! hg6 32 Rd7 etc.

29 ef6 Bf3 30 gf3 Qf6 31 Rc1!

This switch heralds a decisive penetration.

31...Qf3 32 Rc8 Kf7 33 Qg5!

Threatening mate with 34 Rc7 etc.

35...Nc6 34 Rc7 Kf8

34...Ke8 35 Rc6 Qc6 36 Bb5.

35 Be4! (Diagram 46)

Here we have a good example of a piece being 'overloaded' as Black's queen has too much responsibility.

35... Qd1

Black has a final throw of the dice with a trick that I only noted afterwards – namely 35...Ra5. Then 36 d5! looks like a good counter.

36 Kg2 1-0

Black lost on time.

Chapter Two

The King in the Centre

We are told to try to castle the king away to 'safety' as early as possible – otherwise unpleasant things might happen. It is not just that the corners are safer areas, for there is also – very often – the additional problem of incomplete mobilisation of the defender's forces as in most cases a king under attack in the centre is one which never lived anywhere else. Certainly, in this selection of attacks from my games the king is caught where it started the game.

 TIP: To keep the enemy king in the centre – without necessarily opening up the position nor inflicting structural harm – it is often worth material investment.

A good example is Game 8 where an initial sacrifice of a pawn is followed by one of a bishop – primarily to keep the black king where it may be shot at. We have essentially the same scenario in Game 11.

In Game 12 Black throws in a knight to make the white king stay on d1, and it is a similar story in Game 13. In Game 15 an inspired and important theoretical novelty that involves a pawn sacrifice pins the black king in the middle, where an opening of lines soon finishes him off.

Finally, in Game 16 Black is nailed down – in a manner I have never seen elsewhere – by white knights at e6 and b6. These proved so powerful that White, quite correctly, eschewed trading one of them in for a mere exchange, and instead used them as the basis for a crushing assault.

Game 8
□ **Plaskett** ■ **Turner**
Nottingham Open 1997

I had an idea in the 4 a3 variation of the Queens Indian Defence. I first used it to win a game against Keith Arkell in a blitz tournament in Coventry in 1982 and then unleashed it, again with success, on Paul Littlewood at the 1984 Northampton Open. But neither of these games was well-publicised and, 16 years after I first thought of it, it was to make its most emphatic appearance...

1 d4 Nf6 2 c4 e6 3 Nf3 b6 4 a3 c5 5 d5 Ba6 6 Nc3!? (Diagram 1)

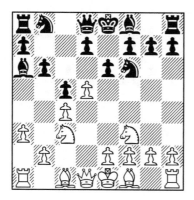
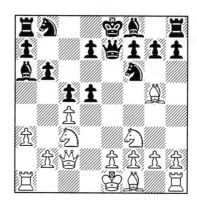

Diagram 1	**Diagram 2**
A gambit try	Kasparov's idea

The idea may have been influenced by the novelty I had seen Kasparov use against van der Wiel at the World Under-26 Team Championships in Graz in 1981: 6 Qc2 Qe7 7 Bg5 ed5 8 Nc3!! **(Diagram 2)**

This should have led to a big advantage but, in fact, Kasparov mishandled the early middlegame and John even got an edge, although normal service was resumed and White won. A few days later van der Wiel told me he thought 8 Nc3!! was a crushing novelty.

6...Bc4

Declining with 6...ed5 may be better.

7 e4 Bf1

7...ed5 8 Bc4 dc4 9 e5 would grant White healthy compensation for a pawn (the one at c4 is a goner) in the form of development and space.

8 Rf1

I argued that for his pawn White has space, a development lead and some light squares in Black's camp at which to aim. In this game we shall see the rook's arrival on the f-file also playing an important role.

8...d6

A theoretical novelty. In reply to 8...ed5 9 e5! Qe7? 10 Qe2 White is clearly better, while 9...d4 10 ef6 Qf6 11 Bg5! Qe6 12 Kd2! dc3 13 Kc3 leaves Black with no defence against the coming Re1. Also good for White is 10...Qc6 11 Qe2 Qe6 12 Nd5 Bd6 13 Bf4 etc.

Littlewood had tried 8...a6 but after 9 Bf4 he should not have equalised. 9 Bg5 and 9 d6 are also worthy of exploration. I forget the Arkell game.

8...b5!? was tried when Boris Gulko scooped up my novelty to score a quick victory against Nisipeanu in the USA-Romania match of the 1998 Olympiad, and it met with the inferior (in my opinion) response of 9 Nb5 Qa5 10 Nc3 Ne4, when Black had reasonable chances of mixing it. Again 9 Bg5 or 9 d6 would be my proposed alternatives.

9 de6 fe6 10 Qb3

Later Grandmaster Speelman preferred 10 e5?! in his game with Romanishin from an England–Ukraine match, afterwards explaining to me that he thought it to be the main line and that he didn't know anything about the theory of this game! He got little after 10...de5 11 Qd8 Kd8 and the game was quickly drawn.

10...Qc8

10...d5 11 Bg5 would leave Black hamstrung and 10...Qd7 invites 11 e5 with increased effect after 11...de5 12 Ne5, while after 11...Ng4 White may try for an edge with 12 ed6 Bd6 13 Bg5!? and a rapid Rd1 (or even 0-0-0) to follow.

10...e5 leaves gaping holes on the light squares as well as presenting White with attacking potential, as evinced in a line like 11 Bg5 Be7 12 0-0-0 Nc6 13 Ne5!? Ne5 14 f4 with initiative and attack.

11 Bf4 Nc6

Now after 11...e5 12 0-0-0!? ef4 White has is a valid attacking idea in 13 e5. Note that 11...c4? 12 Qb5 leaves White better. One of my pupils, Dr Antonio Palma, suggested 11...Nh5!? here, and this looks like a very interesting possibility.

12 0-0-0 e5 (Diagram 3)

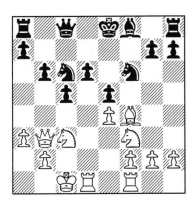

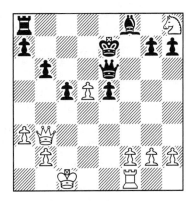

Diagram 3
Time for a breakthrough

Diagram 4
Can Black get the knight?

White might now perhaps claim slight positional compensation after 13 Bg5 Nd4 14 Qc4 thanks to the hole on d5.

13 Be5!!

But blasting our way in is much more fun.

13...de5

Or 13...Ne5 14 Ne5 Ne5 15 f4 and the rook's recapturing at f1 is revealed as ideal as the f-file opens and Black cannot hope to resist.

14 Ng5

Hitting f7 – the classical square to aim at.

14...Nd8

This retreat is necessary since 14...Qc7? allows 15 Qe6 etc.

15 f4!?

Opening the f-file, bringing the f1 rook into the fray and introducing the possibility of using the pawns as attackers. 15 Rd8 was certainly an option, when after 15...Kd8 (15...Qd8?? 16 Qf7 mate)16 Nf7 Ke7 17 Nh8 Qe6 White could maintain the momentum of attack with 18 Nd5 Nd5 19 ed5 (**Diagram 4**). Then after 19...Qh6 20 Kb1 White has at his disposal the remarkable device of d5-d6, bringing the knight on h8 back into the game. It is not clear that White's attack has stopped, for if Black blocks with 20...Qd6 there comes 21 Qf3.

15...Nd7!

Black finds an ingenious defence. 15...c4 16 Qb5 Nc6 17 Qc4 wins for White, as does 15...Qc6 16 fe5 c4 17 Qb5.

16 fe5 c4!

16...Be7 17 Ne6 Ne6 18 Qe6 Rf8 19 Nd5 and the defences collapse, e.g. 19...Qd8 20 Rf8. Turner's choice makes things much tougher for me.

17 Qb5 Be7!

Again the best move as others fail to stave off the attack, e.g. 17...Qc6 18 e6 Qb5 19 Nb5 with threats to d7 and c7, or 17...a6 18 Qd5 Qc6 19 e6 Nf6 20 Qf5 Be7 21 Nh7! and access (via g6) to f7 decides.

18 e6!

Donating an important attacking unit to co-ordinate my army.

18...Bg5 19 Qg5 Ne6 20 Qh5!

A crucial finesse that further softens up the defences, depriving Black's knight of the f6-square.

20... g6 21 Qd5 Ndc5 22 Nb5

Another attacker is called up.

22...Ke7 23 Qd6 Ke8 24 Qd5 Ke7 25 Qd6 Ke8 (Diagram 5)

So, we know the draw is there – should White be content to split the point. Note that 26 Qe5 Nd3 is annoying. Not long before this game I had read a piece by Yusupov in which he said that he had noted that, at the height of an attack, Kasparov would often make a quiet move with his king. That helped to lead me to...

26 Kb1!

White has the time to set up Qe5 without the check on d3.

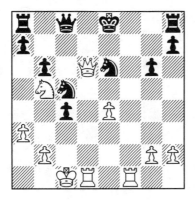

Diagram 5
Should White take the draw?

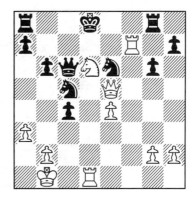

Diagram 6
White powers through

26...Rg8

After 26...a6 27 Qe5 Black is unable to deal with the dual threats of the fork on d6 and the capture on h8. Meanwhile, 26...Rf8 27 Nc7! sees Black overloaded (27...Qc7 28 Rf8), and on 26...Qb8 27 Qc6 Ke7 the knight flicks back into the attack from another square with 28 Nc3!, when Black is defenceless to its arrival on d5.

27 Qe5

Vacating d6, with tempo, for the arrival of the knight. This decides the game.

27...Qc6 28 Nd6 Kd8 29 Rf7 (Diagram 6) 29...Ne4 30 Ne4 Ke8 31 Nd6 Qd6 32 Rd6 Kf7 33 Rd7 Kf8 34 Qd6 Ke8 35 Qe7 mate.

Game 9
☐ **Plaskett** ■ **Holmes**
British Championship, Swansea 1987

1 e4 c5 2 Nc3 Nc6 3 f4 e6 4 Nf3 a6

A good treatment, for White now has nothing better than to go into a main line of the Sicilian Taimanov. My game from the last round of the 1978 British Championship, where I finished second, was against William Watson, who would win the title himself in 1994. It went 4...Nge7 5 g3 g6 6 d4 cd4 7 Nd4 Bg7 8 Be3 0-0 9 Bg2 Qb6 10 e5 Qb2 11 Ndb5 Qb4 12 Rb1 Qa5 13 Bd2 Nf5 14 Ne4 Qa2 15 0-0 f6 16 g4 Nfe7 17 ef6 Bf6 18 Nf6 Rf6 19 Bc3 Rf8 **(Diagram 7)** 20 f5 Qc4 21 f6 Qc5 22 Kh1 Nd5 23 f7 Rf7 24 Rf7 Kf7 25 Qf3 Kg8 26 Rf1 Qe7 **(Diagram 8)** 27 Qd5 ed5 28 Bd5 Qe6 29 Nc7 Rb8 30 g5 Ne7 31 Be6 de6 32 Be5 Bd7 33 Nd5 Nd5 34 Bb8 a6 35 Bd6 Bc6 36 Kg1 Ne3 37 Rf8 Kg7 38 Rb8 Nc2 39 Be5 Kf7 40 Rh8 Nc2 41 Rh7 Kd8 42 Kf2 Nb4 43 Bd6 Nd5 44 h4 Be8 45 Rb7 a5 46 Rg7 a4 47 Ke2 Kc8 48 Kd3 a3 49 Ba3 Nf4 50 Ke4 Ng2 51 Rh7 1-0. Ah, those were the days!

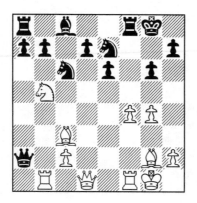

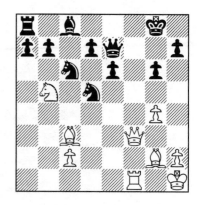

Diagram 7
How to attack here?

Diagram 8
Can you spot White's next?

5 d4

Against Portisch in an active game from Oviedo, 1993, I tried 5 g3 d5 6 Bg2 d4 7 Ne2 d3! 8 cd3 Qd3 9 Ne5 Ne5 10 fe5, and I even managed to win from that dubious start.

5...cd4 6 Nd4 Nge7 7 Be3 d5!?

This is definitely not a Taimanov move, yet by no means out of the question, nonetheless. 7...b5, 7...Nd4, 7...Ng6 and 7...d6 were all more regular.

8 Nc6!? bc6 9 Qd2

Often when White takes on c6 in the Taimanov he seeks to demonstrate that Black's ...a7-a6 then serves no purpose.

9...Qa5?!

This did not work out well.

10 0-0-0 Bb7 11 Kb1 c5?!

It is certainly unwise to initiate action when behind in development, although White needs to find the refutation at move 13.

12 ed5 ed5 (Diagram 9) 13 Bc4!

The beginning of Black's problems.

13...d4

13...0-0-0? 14 Nd5 Qd2 15 Ne7 Be7 16 Rd2 Rd2 17 Bd2 Bg2 18 Rg1 and White wins.

14 f5!

Vacating the f4-square for the bishop and perhaps intending to use the f-pawn itself in the attack.

14...Bc6

Now 14...0-0-0 is met by 15 Bf7 so that either capture by the d4-pawn runs into the check on e6, picking up the rook.

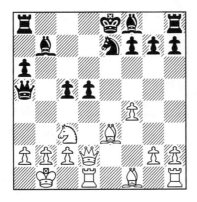

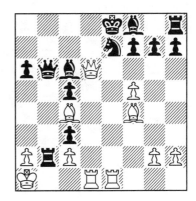

Diagram 9
How to develop the f1-bishop?

Diagram 10
Whose attack is stronger?

15 Rhe1 Rb8

15...0-0-0 still allows 16 Bf7!, while after 15...dc3 16 Qd6 Black will never survive against the concentration of central firepower.

16 Bf4! dc3

By now Black might as well take his chances.

17 Qd6 Rb2 18 Ka1 Qb6 (Diagram 10) 19 Rb1

Black threatened to deliver mate on b2 after an initial check on a2.

WARNING: In any attack we must always also consider the safety of our own king.

In this case the development lead plus my entire army taking aim at Black's open king position means that the loss of a minor piece matters little.

19...f6 20 Qe6 Bg2 21 Qc8 Qd8 22 Bf7 Kf7 23 Qd8 Nf5 24 Qe8 1-0

Because chess starts from a fixed position it is possible to subject the openings to concrete analysis. In 1985 Vaganian told me that in his opinion when you reach World Championship level chess is almost entirely about opening theory. In exceptional instances the play becomes so sharp so early on that, indeed, the entire struggle may reside in the first moves. Here are two *theoretical* attacks against a future British Champion.

Game 10
□ **Plaskett** ■ **Gallagher**
A.R.C. Masters, Chichester 1982

1 e4 c5 2 Nf3 d6 3 d4 cd4 4 Nd4 Nf6 5 Nc3 a6 6 Bg5 e6 7 f4 b5 (Diagram 11)

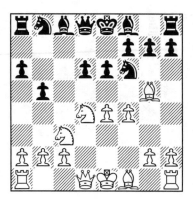

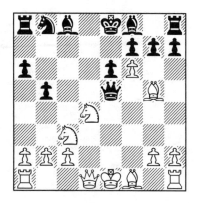

Diagram 11
A very sharp line

Diagram 12
Regaining the piece

The Polugaevsky Variation, one of the sharpest and most theoretical opening lines.

8 e5 de5 9 fe5 Qc7 10 ef6

10 Qe2 is the other main line.

10...Qe5 (Diagram 12)

Lev's point: Black gets back his piece.

11 Be2 Qg5 12 0-0 Qe5

This is esoteric stuff but is long supported by theory and analysis. Later that year Joe played the innovation 12...Qe3?! against me, when there followed 13 Kh1 gf6 (**Diagram 13**)

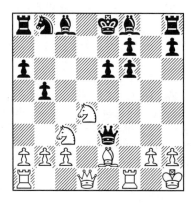

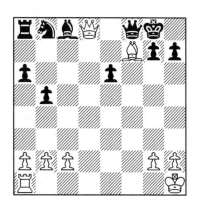

Diagram 13
What is best here?

Diagram 14
A nice tactic

I then played the stupid 14 Qe1? Nd7 15 Rd1 and lost in 27 moves. When Gallagher subsequently showed what he thought to be an important novelty to GM Nunn, it took the Doctor less than a minute to demonstrate that 14 Nd5! ed5 15 Qd5 leaves White with a big advantage.

13 Nf3 Bc5 14 Kh1 Qf6

Extensive analysis, even before the advent of computer analysis engines, established that these were amongst the sharpest and most accurate moves for each side in the positions stemming from Black's 7th move.

15 Ne4 Qe7 16 Nfg5 f5

Polugaevsky himself had suffered one of his rare losses in his own variation in a game with Beliavsky after 16...0-0 17 Nf7!, the point being that 17...Rf7 18 Rf7 Kf7 19 Bh5 exposes a check on f3 to pick off the a8-rook, and retreating with 19...Kg8 allows the fiendish 20 Nc5 Qc5? 21 Qd8 Qf8 22 Bf7! (**Diagram 14**). Consequently 16...f5 became the recommendation, but not to castle may in itself bring problems.

17 b4

My baby. In a game from earlier that year in Telford I had played the theoretically recommended 17 Bh5 against Joe and after 17...g6 18 Nh7 Kf7! (taking on h7 opens a can of worms, so this is more rational) 19 Nhg5 Kg7 20 Nc5 Qc5 21 Bf3 Qe5? (an unguarded moment; simply 21...Ra7 is fine) 22 h3 Ra7 23 Re1 Qf6 24 Ne6! Be6 25 Re6 Qe6 26 Qd4 Qf6 27 Qa7 (loose pieces drop off) 27...Kh6 28 Re1 Qd6 29 Qe3 f4 30 Qf2 Nc6 31 Bc6 Qc6 32 Qh4 Kg7 33 Qe7 Kh6 34 Re6 and Black resigned.

17...Bb4 18 Bh5 g6 19 Nh7 Kf7 20 Rf5 (Diagram 15)

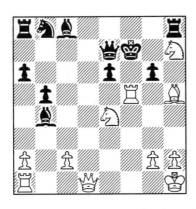

Diagram 15
White has very active minor pieces!

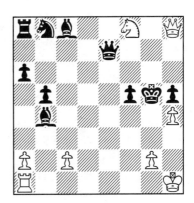

Diagram 16
The game is up

This is certainly livelier than last time!

20...ef5 21 Neg5 Kg7?

Black could very satisfactorily deal with my novelty with 21...Kg8! 22

Qd5 Be6! etc. Now, however, the end is nigh.

22 Qd4 Kh6 23 Qh8 gh5

23...Qg7 24 Nf7! Qf7 25 Nf6 Kg5 26 h4! Kf4 27 Rf1 is awful for Black.

24 Nf8! Kg5 25 h4! 1-0 (Diagram 16)

After 25...Kg4 26 Qg8 Black cannot avoid the deadly fork on g6.

In the next game it was I who faced a theoretical novelty, one which is still being debated twenty years later.

Game 11
☐ **Plaskett** ■ **Murei**
Gausdal 1985

1 Nf3 c5 2 e4 Nc6 3 Bb5 Nf6 4 Nc3 e5!? (Diagram 17)

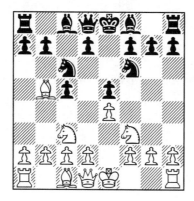
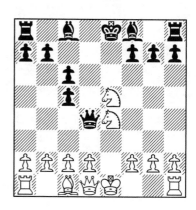

| **Diagram 17** | **Diagram 18** |
| An interesting try | Black regains the knight |

This is the new move, inviting a flurry of trades in the centre.

5 Bc6 dc6 6 Ne5 Ne4! 7 Ne4 Qd4 (Diagram 18)

The point – Black regains his knight.

8 Qe2 Qe5 9 f4 Qf4!?

And this amazing move quite shocked me. I then saw that after 10 Nf6 Kd8 11 Qe8 Kc7 12 Qf7 Kd8! the game ends in a forced draw. Consequently I chose the next active move.

10 d4 Qh4 11 g3 Qe7 12 Bg5

White continues to gain time on the busy queen.

12...f6

12...Qe6 might have been less hazardous, although White would still have a lot of play for his pawn after 13 0-0.

13 0-0-0!

A thinking-feeling move. I saw quite a few of the most important variations, but I do not believe that anyone could calculate everything here.

13...fg5

After the game when looking at 13...Bd7 Murei demonstrated a fine variation: 14 dc5 0-0-0 15 Nd6 and Black loses prosaically after 15...Kb8 16 Qe7 Be7 17 Nf7, or beautifully after 17...Kc7 18 Bf4!! Qe2 19 Nb5 Kc8 20 Na7 mate. Given that Black is unable to castle his way to safety he must instead fight it out with his king in the centre.

14 dc5

A development lead and the opponent's king stuck in the middle constitute classical compensation. But a piece is a piece.

14...Qe5

This is as good a way as any of coping with the threat of Nd6, as can be seen from the following:

a) 14...Qe6 15 Rhe1 Be7 16 Nd6 Bd6 17 Qh5 g6 18 Re6 Be6 19 Qe2 and White wins.

b) 14...Kf7 is well motivated, but after 15 Rhf1 Kg8 there comes 16 Rd6!, an idea with which I was very pleased during the game. White threatens 17 Qc4, and Black cannot deal with it by either 16...h6 17 Qc4 Kh7 18 Rf7 and 19 Nf6, or 16...Be6 17 Re6! Qe6 18 Nf6! Qf6 19 Qc4 and mate.

15 Rhe1 (Diagram 19)

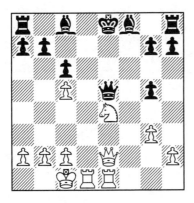 

Diagram 19	**Diagram 20**
With some central pressure...	What is the most accurate move?

Renewing the threat to jump in on d6 as well as introducing the possibility of sending the queen to h5.

15...Be6!

Again Black finds the best chance. In reply to 15...Bc5 White has 16 Nf6! gf6 17 Qh5 and Black will be forced to concede material or expose his king to a terrible attack, for example:

a) 17...Kf8 18 Re5 fe5 19 Rd8 Kg7 20 Qg5.

b) 17...Ke7 18 Re5 fe5 19 Qg5 and Black will now lose one of his un-protected pieces on c5 or h8, after 19...Kf7 20 Rf1, or 19...Ke6 20 Qh5 Kf5 (20...Kf7 21 Rf1 Ke8 22 Qh5 and 23 Qe5 forks c5 and h8) 21 Rf1 Ke4 and a king hunt will end in a line such as 22 Qh4 Ke3 23 Re1 Kf2 24 g4 Kg2 25 Qg3 mate.

16 Qh5! g6!

Yet another best move. 16...Bf7 sees Black lose material after 17 Nd6 Bd6 18 Qg5.

17 Qg5 Qg5 18 Ng5 Bh6 19 Re6 Kf8

White's imaginative attacking play has yielded him a won game.

20 h4?!

As the subject of this book is attack I shall not dwell too long on my technical inaccuracies which now ensued. A stronger route here would begin with 20 Rf1.

20...Bg5 21 hg5 Re8 22 Rf6 Ke7 (Diagram 20)

23 Rdf1?

Clearly best was 23 Rdd6!, intending Kd2, Kd3 and then the launch of the queenside pawns. In fact that should win, but after the text Murei seized his chance and defended well.

23...Kd8 24 Rd6 Kc8 25 Rf7 Ref8 26 R7f6 Rf6 27 gf6 h5 28 Kd2 g5 29 Re6?

29 Ke3! is preferable, although Black should still hold with 29...Re8! 30 Kf3 Re1! etc.

29...h4 30 gh4 gh4 31 Re7 h3 32 f7 Rd8 33 Kc3 h2 34 Re8 h1Q 35 Rd8 Kd8 36 f8Q Kc7 37 Qd6 Kc8 and a draw was agreed.

Game 12
□ **McDonald** ■ **Plaskett**
Hampstead 1998

---

1 e4 c5 2 Nf3 e6 3 d4 cd4 4 Nd4 Nc6 5 Nb5

One of the main lines, but it does move a developed piece twice.

5...d6

I once invented the move 5...Bc5 here – or I thought I did. Murei later told me that he had played it years before in the U.S.S.R. I beat Med-nis with it, and managed draws with Chandler and Judit Polgar, but savage defeats at the hands of Mokry and Gufeld put me off and no-body plays it these days. My favourite game with 5...Bc5 was from the 1984 British Zonal when I played Comben. The game went 6 Bf4 Qf6 7 Bg3 (7 Qc1!) 7...h5!? 8 h4 Nh6!? 9 Nc7 Kd8 10 Na8 Ng4 11 f3 Ne3 **(Diagram 21)**

Now White played the bizarre 12 Bc7?, but the critical line is 12 Qc1 Nd4 13 Na3 Nf3 14 gf3 Qf3 15 Rg1 Qe4 16 Be2 Nf5 **(Diagram 22)**

This position actually occurred in a game I played as Black against

Peter Large in a 1981 quickplay, and I went on to win. The critical lines stem from 17 Bf2 (which he did not play) 17...Bf2 18 Kf2 when Black can consider 18...Qh4, 18...Rh6 and 18...b5. The game with Comben did not go much further: 12...Ke8 13 e5 Qf4 14 Qd2 Nd4 15 Rh3 Ndc2 16 Ke2 b6 17 Qd3 Nd4 18 Ke1 Ndc2 19 Ke2 Nf1 20 Nd2 Ba6 and White resigned.

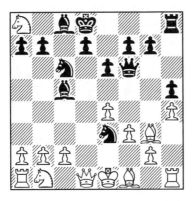

Diagram 21
A fine mess

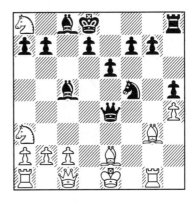

Diagram 22
Another fine mess

6 Bf4 e5 7 Be3 Be6 8 Nd2 Nf6 9 Bg5 Be7 10 Bf6 Bf6! 11 Nc4 (Diagram 23)

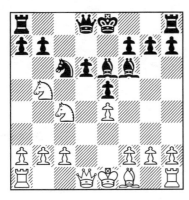

Diagram 23
Targetting the d-pawn

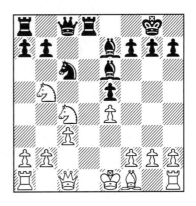

Diagram 24
Black has good play for the pawn

11...0-0

Thus Black gambits, but he receives excellent compensation in activity. Indeed, this whole line is a non-starter for White as a winning attempt.

12 Qd6 Qc8 13 c3

A well-motivated follow-up, White wanting to cover d4.

13...Be7 14 Qd2

Four years later Luke McShane preferred 14 Qd1 against me in a game from the Redbus Knockout, which continued 14...Rd8 15 Qc1 **(Diagram 24)**

Now Black may equalise via 15...Bc4 16 Bc4 a6 17 Na3 Ba3 18 ba3 Qg4, but I preferred some merry mayhem and opted for 15...Nb4! 16 Ne5 (the best chance as after 16 Nba3 Black might even investigate 16...b5!?, e.g. 17 Nb5 Bc4 18 Na7 Qg4 19 Bc4 Qg2 20 Rf1 Bg5 and wins) 16...Bg5! 17 f4 and at the cost of his f-pawn White found sanctuary for his king and improved co-ordination: 17...Bf4 18 Qf4 Nc2 19 Kf2 Qc5 20 Kg3 and, as Luke remarked afterwards, his king is actually reasonably secure here. The win for Black is now on material rather than further attack. The game continued 20...Na1 21 b4, when the simplest line is 21...Qe7! 22 Be2 Nc2 23 Rc1 g5! 24 Qf3 Rd2 and the newly arrived rook serves to hang on to the knight and so retain Black's material lead. Sadly, I made several inaccuracies and actually went on to lose.

14...Rd8 15 Qe3 (Diagram 25)

Diagram 25
Black has good play

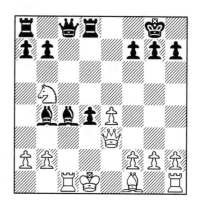

Diagram 26
Can White exploit the pin?

Again Black could equalise completely by 15...Bc4 16 Bc4 a6 17 Na3 Ba3.

15...Nd4!?

But this is much more fun.

16 cd4 Bc4 17 Rc1

Neither 17 d5 f5 nor 17 de5 Bb5 18 Bb5 Qc2 are clearly favourable for White, although the latter involves little risk.

17...Bb4!

The point of Black's sacrifice: he will generate play against the white king.

18 Kd1 ed4 (Diagram 26) 19 Nd4?

A blunder. The most demanding analysis stems from attempting to make something of the pin on the bishop on c4, e.g. 19 Qg5 d3 20 b3 f6! 21 Qh5 Bf7 and Black escapes, or 21 Qe3 Bb5! 22 Rc8 Rac8 and Black's attack is decisive. Also in need of investigation is 19 Qf4 d3 20 e5 (**Diagram 27**)

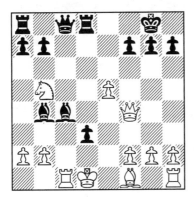

Diagram 27
How to break the pin?

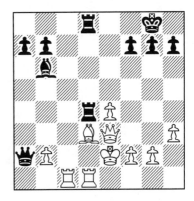

Diagram 28
Black has a good initiative

I at first thought that Black might 'bail out' here with 20...Bb5 21 Rc8 Rac8 22 Qb4 d2 when, following the capture of the d2-pawn, Black's initiative would fully compensate, e.g. 23 Qd2 Rd2 24 Kd2 Rd8 25 Kc1 Rc8 26 Kb1 Bc6 27 f3 Re8 28 f4 Be4 etc.

Alternatively it is possible for White to steer the game to a position with his queen versus my two rooks with 23 Bb5 Rc1 24 Ke2 Rh1 25 Ba4, and here it is not out of the question that White might yet keep an edge in a plausible continuation such as 25...b6 26 Qe7 d1Q 27 Bd1 Rhd1 28 Qa7.

20...Ba2!? is much more interesting as 21 Rc8? loses to 21...Bb3! and 21 Qb4 grants Black excellent attacking compensation for a piece after 21...Qf5.

19...Bc5?

The simple 19...b5! wins thanks to White's insuperable problems with his king and the pinned knight, e.g. 20 Bc4 bc4 21 Rc2 Qc5, or 21 a3 when at least 21...Ba3 and 22...Qc5 will do the job. Here 21 Ke2 runs into 21...Qa6! with multiple threats of 22...c3, 22...Qa2 and 22...Bc5, White's best option perhaps being 22 Rcd1 Qa2 23 Kf3 Qb2 and Black is winning.

En passant, note that the attack against the king in the centre is so strong that Black might be able to get away with even 19...Ba2!?, e.g. 20 Rc8 Rac8 when he threatens (amongst others) 20...Bc5, so White will have to give back the knight with something like 21 Bd3 Bc5, and Black is no worse.

20 Bc4?

Failing to exploit my error! He had 20 Rc4 b5 21 Rc2!, a move we had both quite overlooked, and his pin against my queen means that Black has no advantage at all!

20...Rd4?

The fourth consecutive mistake. 20...Bd4! was best after which White is clearly lost. He cannot escape after 21 Bf7 Kf7 22 Qb3 Qe6 23 Rc7 when nimble footwork will see Black safely home after 23...Kf6 24 Qf3 Kg6 25 Qg3 Kh5 and wins. Nor does 21 Bd5 help: 21...Be3 22 Rc8 Rac8 23 fe3 Rc4! 24 Ke2 Rc2 25 Kf3 Kf8 etc.

21 Bd3 Qg4 22 Kd2!

With an irritating attack on c5 McDonald defends well.

22...Bb6

Despite his two glaring mistakes Black retains good prospects. White's king is still unsafe and, as Botvinnik pointed out, when there are opposite coloured bishops a player with the attack is essentially a piece up.

23 h3 Qe6 24 Ke2 Rad8 25 Rhd1 Qa2 (Diagram 28)

Re-establishing material parity, and keeping the initiative.

26 Rc2 h6 27 Qc1 Qe6 28 Rc3 Qf6

A probing move that keeps White on his toes.

29 Rf1 Qg6

Continuing to harass White, the text concentrates on the soft spots at e4 and g2.

30 Qf4 Qg2 31 Qg4 Qh2 32 Qg3

Note that 32 Rg1 invites 32...Re4!, when f2 is about to fall.

32...Qg3 33 fg3 Kf8

Black is technically winning.

34 Rb3 Ke7 35 Rf5 R8d7 36 Re5 Kd8 37 Bb5 Re7 38 Re7 Ke7 39 Kf3 Rd2 0-1

White lost on time.

Game 13
□ **Agnos** ■ **Plaskett**
British Championship, Southampton 1986

Dmitrios Agnos lived in England for a while before qualifying as a GM and then returning to his native Greece.

1 e4 d6 2 d4 Nf6 3 Nc3 g6 4 Bg5 Nbd7?! (Diagram 29)

This particular move order is not highly regarded by theory.

5 f4 h6 6 Bh4 Bg7 7 e5?!

Advancing here is rather over-exuberant, and instead the simple 7 Nf3! would leave Black struggling to find a path to equality.

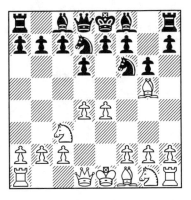

Diagram 29
Provocative

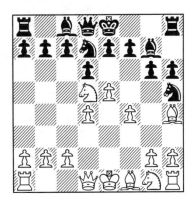

Diagram 30
Very provocative

7...Nh5 8 Nd5 (Diagram 30)

Threatening the queen by hitting e7, but Black's natural reply effectively addresses the issue at hand.

8...c6! 9 Ne7

Now 9 Be7? sees White come unstuck thanks to the check on a5.

9...de5 10 fe5

This time 10 Ng6? falls short to the check.

10...Qb6

Black generates excellent activity and a development lead as compensation for his pawn.

11 b3?!

Gambiting with 11 Nf3 was more practical. After the text 11...c5! is logical and good, but I thought I spotted something even more interesting.

11...Ne5!?

The point is that 12 de5 allows 11...Qb4 followed by picking up the loose bishop on h4... loose pieces drop off.

12 Nc8 Rc8 13 Qd2! (Diagram 31)

Now the speculative 13...0-0!? 14 de5 Be5 is by no means out of the question but, again, I found something even more interesting.

13...Ng4! 14 Qe2

If White does not take the bait Black has a very healthy game, although 14 0-0-0! was a better chance.

14...Kf8 15 Qg4??

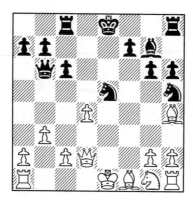

Diagram 31
White has terrible development

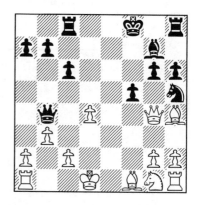

Diagram 32
Only the king and queen are developed

This loses outright. After 15 Be7 Kg8 16 Bc5 Black has 15...Qa5 16 b4 Qa3, when 17 Qg4 is still losing thanks to 17...Qc3, e.g. 18 Kf2 Re8 and a1 drops. Instead 15 0-0-0, *which would have got his king out of the centre*, was still best, when Black stands well after he pulls a knight back to f6.

15... Qb4 16 Kd1 f5! 0-1 (Diagram 32)

White is a full piece up but quite defenceless. In reply to 16 Qg6 Black has 16...Qd4, and in the event of 16 Be1 Black has the strong 16...Qe1 17 Ke1 fg4 or 16...Qb6!, which maintains the attack on d4 and wins.

13...Ng4! proved an unusual decoy.

In the following game I was very pleased with my creative achievement in adding something valuable to a main line, although the story was to have a little twist.

Game 14
☐ **Plaskett** ■ **Hartston**
ARC Masters, Uppingham 1986

1 e4 c5 2 Nf3 e6 3 d4 cd4 4 Nd4 Nc6 5 Nc3 a6 6 Be2 Nge7 7 0-0 Nd4 8 Qd4 Nc6 9 Qd3 Nb4?! (Diagram 33)

Plaskett-Speelman, Aaronson Masters 1979 had continued 9...Qc7 10 Be3 b5 11 f4 Bb7 12 Rad1 Be7 13 a4 Nb4!? 14 Qd2 Nc2 15 Qc2 b4 16 Rd4 and now Black tried 16...d5?!, a little too clever considering his lagging development and the king being still in the centre. There followed 17 ed5 Bd5 18 Bc4! bc3 (18...Bc4 19 Ne4 Rc8 20 Rc1 and the pin decides.) 19 Qc3 Qb7 20 Rfd1 Bc6 **(Diagram 34)** 21 f5! ef5 22 Rd6! Bd6 23 Rd6 (threatening 24 Rc6) 24...0-0 25 Rc6 and Black had paid the price for leaving his king in the centre, where it became exposed to attack (1-0, 35). 9...Nb4 had been played twice by Taimanov himself versus Karpov and Kiril Georgiev, with White, in each instance, retreating his queen to d2 and following up with the fianchetto of his queen's bishop.

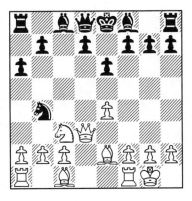

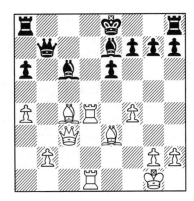

Diagram 33	**Diagram 34**
A knight sortie	White is on the attack

Over the board, I spotted a new and much more vigorous idea.

10 Qg3! Nc2

Since Black cannot develop his kingside he might as well take the pawn.

11 Bg5! f6 12 Bf4!

The point is that 12...Na1? loses to 13 Bh5 g6 (13...Ke7 14 Bd6 mate) 14 Bg6 hg6 15 Qg6 Ke7 16 e5! d5 17 Qf6 Kd7 18 Qh8 when Black is unable to extricate his knight with 18...Nc2 in view of 19 Qh7, picking it up.

12...Kf7

Here Bill Hartston whimsically commented 'I know it's bad manners, but I offer a draw'...

13 Bc7! Qe8

After 13...Qe7 14 Rad1 White would also have excellent compensation, although this might be preferable to the text.

14 Rad1

White has Na4-b6 in mind, hence Black's next.

14...b5 (Diagram 35)

15 e5!

With this decisive thrust, White steps up the pace.

15...Bb7

16...fe5 loses to 17 Qf3, while 15...f5 16 Bf3 Ra7 17 Bb6 Rb7 18 Bb7 Bb7 19 Qd3 also wins for White.

16 ef6 Kg8

16...gf6 17 Bh5 Ke718 Qd6 mate. The alternative 16...Kf6 fails to 17 Be5 Kf7 18 Bh5 g6 19 Qf4 Kg8 20 Qf6, and 16...g6 meets with 17 Qd3.

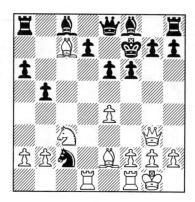

Diagram 35
How to get at the king?

Diagram 36
Loose pieces drop off

17 fg7 Bg7 18 Be5 1-0 (Diagram 36)

After 18...Qg6 19 Qg6 hg6 20 Bg7 Kg7 21 Rd7 White picks up the bishop.

I was proud of my new idea, yet imagine my surprise a fortnight later when Nigel Davies told me that he had also discovered 10 Qg3! and had been intending to use it against Taimanov himself in a Lisbon tournament, but the master had varied with 6...Qc7.

There have been no master games since with 9...Nb4.

Remarking on Kasparov's quick win against Marjanovic at the 1980 Malta Olympiad, GM Michael Stean noted that it showed just '...how vulnerable a GM can be once out of his insulating coat of opening theory.' In our next game it was not so much that there was anything new about my opening moves; rather it was the whole system with which my opponent was unfamiliar.

Game 15
☐ **Plaskett** ■ **Shipov**
Hastings 2000

1 e4 c5 2 Nc3 d6 3 f4 Nc6 4 Nf3 g6 5 Bb5

This is probably superior to 5 Bc4.

5... Bd7!

Black does not want to allow the doubling of his pawns.

6 0-0 Bg7 7 d3 a6 8 Bc6 Bc6 9 Kh1 Qd7 10 Qe2

A natural move in appearance, but in fact games with Qe1 were far more common.

10...f5?

This thrust is the cause of all Black's troubles. Instead 10...Nf6, 10...e6, 10...0-0-0 and 10...Nh6 were all superior.

11 Nd5! (Diagram 37)

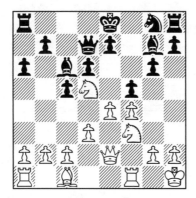

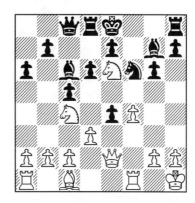

Diagram 37
A knight thrust

Diagram 38
Another knight thrust

Heralding the beginning of two remarkable knight tours.

11...Rd8

Preparing to evict the knight now that there is no fork on b6.

12 Ng5!

A further, uncompromising knight advance, the point being that on 12...e6 I simply take it thanks to another fork on c7.

12...Nf6 13 Nb6! Qc7 14 Nc4 fe4 15 Ne6 Qc8 (Diagram 38)

Now on 16 Ng7 Kf7 the knight is trapped, and 16 Nd8 would let Black off too lightly.

16 f5!

But this is much stronger, offering the knight the exit square on e6 and introducing the f-pawn itself as an attacking unit, in turn focusing on the opening of the f-file.

16...Rg8 17 Nb6!

White has no interest in grabbing a mere exchange and prefers to further harass the queen.

17...ed3 18 cd3 Qb8 19 fg6

Now 19...hg6 19 Ng7 Rg7 20 Rf6 wins for White.

19...Bh8 (Diagram 39) 20 g7!

It is important not to get carried away in this kind of situation – 20 Qh5 works after 20...Nh5 21 gh7 (believe it or not) but 20...hg6 pours cold water on White's creation.

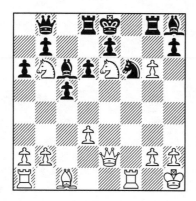

Diagram 39
Two very active knights

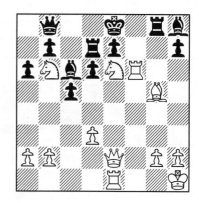

Diagram 40
A killer

WARNING: When executing an attack be wary of fantastic finishes!

20...Bg7

Of White's last ten moves, six were with knights and four with pawns. His queenside is still undeveloped but the inhibitive effect of the two deep sunken knights, is like nothing I ever saw.

21 Bg5 Bh8 22 Rae1 Rd7 23 Rf6! (Diagram 40) 23...ef6

Or 23...Bf6 24 Qh5 Rg6 25 Qh7 and White wins.

24 Nc5 Kd8 25 Ncd7 Bd7 26 Qe7 Kc7 27 Nd5 1-0

Game 16
□ **Plaskett** ■ **Chandler**
British League, Birmingham 2000

1 e4 c5 2 Nc3 e6 3 Nf3 a6 4 d4 cd4 5 Nd4 Qc7 6 Bd3 Nc6 7 Nc6 dc6

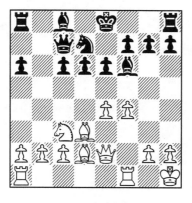

Diagram 41
13 e5 – a classic central thrust

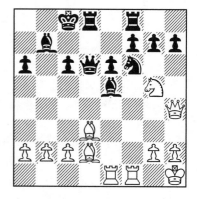

Diagram 42
Black's king is airy

Plaskett-Bezold, Hastings 1997 continued 7...bc6 8 0-0 Nf6 9 Qe2 d6 10 f4 Nd7 11 Kh1 Be7 12 Bd2 Bf6 (**Diagram 41**)

Now it was time for some fun: 13 e5!? de5 14 Ne4 Bb7 15 fe5 Be5 16 Ng5 Rf8 17 Rae1 Qd6 18 Qh5 Nf6 19 Qe2 Nd7 20 Qh5 Nf6 21 Qh4!? (nothing ventured, nothing gained...)

21...0-0-0 (**Diagram 42**) 22 Nf3! Nd7 (Black is understandably mistrustful of opening up the line in front of his king by 22...Bb2) 23 Ne5 Ne5 24 Bf4 f6 25 Be5 fe5 26 Qh7 Rh8 27 Qe4 Rh5 28 Rf7 (**Diagram 43**)

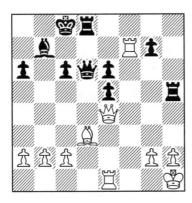

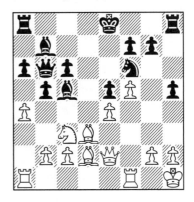

Diagram 43
White is winning

Diagram 44
Black can no longer play ...0-0

White has a totally won game because Black's pieces are poor and structure mangled. However – yet again – time pressure and then my technique let me down and Michael escaped with a draw on the 71st move.

8 0-0 Nf6

8...e5!? is an interesting alternative.

9 f4

Gaining useful space.

9... e5 10 f5

And the further advance adds to White's territorial lead.

10...Bc5 11 Kh1 b5 12 a4

A standard softener with this type of set-up.

12... Bb7 13 Qe2 Qb6

Black prevents the trade of bishops with Be3, but that was not really my intent anyway.

14 Bd2 h5 (Diagram 44)

Despite the fact that the text has its strategical points in that it holds up a possible g2-g4 pawn roller, Black can no longer realistically contemplate castling kingside.

15 Nd1!?

The beginning of an attacking plan – seriously. The queenside pawns are cleared to advance, while the knight has ambitions of its own.

NOTE: Aggressive play can be initiated with a retreat.

15...Qc7 16 b4 Bd4

The attack on the rook is an irrelevance which does nothing to hold back White's queenside.

17 c3 Bb6 18 Nf2 Rd8

Understandably reluctant to castle queenside, Murray improvises. His king may be in the centre, but White's forces are still a long way from this area, and access will necessitate opening lines.

19 Bg5

White had to address the possibility of Black lining up on the d-file with 19...Qd7.

19...Rd6 20 c4 bc4 21 Bc4

Having rather burned his bridges, Black must now cope with his king coming under fire in the centre.

21...Bd4

Although nicely centralised, the influence of this piece turned out to be largely cosmetic. The fight is elsewhere.

22 Rac1 a5 23 ba5 Qa5 24 Rb1 Qa7 25 Bh4!

Another retreat that has an attacking as well as defensive significance, since by dropping back to h4 the bishop leaves g5 available for the knight.

25...Rd7 26 Nh3!? Qa4

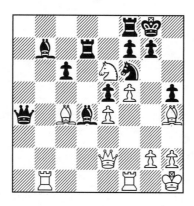

Diagram 45
A knight thrust

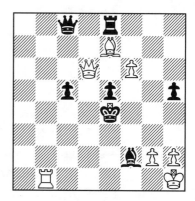

Diagram 46
Black's king is exposed

Black helps himself, but on the other flank White now sends in another (important) attacker.

27 Ng5 Qa8

In the event of 27...0-0 the continuation 28 Nf7!? Rff7 29 Bf6 gf6 30 Bb3 and 31 Qh5 is worth a look, but I had intended 28 Ne6! (**Diagram 45**) Indeed it would seem that the diagram position is hopeless for Black, e.g. 28...fe6 (28...Ba6 29 Ba6 fe6 30 Bc4 wins) 29 fe6 Re7 30 Rb7! Rb7 31 e7 etc.

28 Nf7! Rf8

Played with an audible sigh. However, 28...Rf7 29 Bf7 Kf7 30 Qc4 leads to win of the b7 bishop after 30...Kf8 through 31 Qb4, and moving the king to the e-file permits destruction by 31 Qe6 etc.

29 Ng5

The job is done now as the fall of the f7-pawn leaves Black's king position untenable. The rest of the game is a formality.

29...c5 30 Bb5 Be4 31 Bd7 Kd7 32 Ne4 Ne4 33 Qc4 Kc7 34 Qe6 Re8 35 Qf7 Kc6 36 Be7 Qc8 37 Qg7 Nf2 38 Rf2 Bf2 39 Qf6 Kd5 40 Qd6 Ke4 41 f6 (Diagram 46) 41...Qf5 42 Qc6 Ke3 43 Bc5 Kd2 44 Rb2 Kc3 45 Ba3 1-0

Game 17
□ **Psakhis** ■ **Plaskett**
Bor 1985

At the beginning of the 1980s, Lev Psakhis twice won the Championship of the USSR – an immensely strong tournament. Yet he was destined never to reach the heights his talents demanded, and has not featured as a serious contender for the World Championship.

1 d4 Nf6 2 c4 e6 3 Nc3 Bb4 4 e3 c5 5 Bd3 Nc6 6 a3 Bc3 7 bc3 e5

8...0-0, 8...b6 and 8...d5 are all possibilities here.

8 Ne2

8...d6 has been most often seen, but I wanted to try an idea which Tal had used with success in his game with Spassky from the penultimate round of the USSR Championship of 1958.

8...e4!? 9 Bb1

Afterwards he suggested 9 Bc2, which would have avoided congestion.

9...b6 10 Ng3 Ba6 11 f3!?

11 Ne4 Ne4 12 Be4 Bc4, Martin-Plaskett, Hastings 1985, is equal.

11...Bc4

11...ef3 12 Qf3 activates White's game.

12 fe4

It is better to let him clog himself up a bit by gaining our pawn in this manner. Psakhis here varied from Spassky's play. He had tried 12 Nf5 0-0 13 Nd6 Bd3 14 Bd3 ed3 15 Qd3 cd4 16 cd4 Ne8 17 Nf5 d5 18 a4 Nd6 19 Nd6 Qd6 20 Ba3 Nb4 with equality, although he later over-

overpressed and even lost. In his notes, Tal drew attention to 12 fe4 and recommended a piece sacrifice. I believe that this is the only game where it was tried.

12...d6 13 Qf3 0-0!?

Tal wrote that 13...Rc8 is inferior as 14 Nf5 0-0 15 Qg3 Ne8 16 e5 is better for White. But I beg to differ, so in future we might see games with 13...Rc8.

14 e5 de5

Here I would again disagree with Tal, as it occurs to me that Black is still not obliged to sacrifice, and 14...Nd5!? could be a viable, and perhaps even superior, alternative, e.g. 15 e4 Nde7 15 ed6 Qd6 with White still unable to castle and Black having pressure against the central pawns.

15 Qc6 ed4 (Diagram 47)

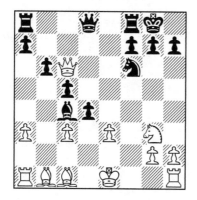

Diagram 47	**Diagram 48**
How to defend?	Three pawns for a rook

'With a strong attack on the king which is caught in the centre.' Tal.

16 cd4?

A weak decision. Other ideas include:

a) 16 ed4? Re8 and Black makes use of the obligingly-opened e-file to prosecute a fierce attack.

b) 16 Ne4 is powerfully met by 16...Nd5! with the idea of ...Qh4.

c) 16 Ba2!? is well-motivated, as it aims to trade off the bishop which is cutting through the white game. After 16...Bd3 play remains obscure.

d) 16 Qf3 is logical as the queen is out of it at c6. Black could consider:

d1) 16...Re8 wheeling another gun out. 17 e4 and now:

d11)17...d3 is best met by 18 Bg5! when White prepares to castle and the tricks after 18...Ne4 are just insufficient for Black after 19 Bd8 Ng5 20 Qe2!, e.g. 20...de2 21 Bg5, or 20...Re2 21 Ne2 Rd8 22 Ng3, or

20...Rad8 21 Qe8, or 20...d2 21 Kd1 Be2 22 Ne2 Rad8 23 Ra2 and Black is not equal.

Alternatively, 19...Ng3 also falls short after 20 Kd1 Bb3 21 Kc1 d2 22 Kb2!, or 20...Nh1 21 Bh4.

d12) 17...dc3 I had been inclined to regard 18 Qc3 as a clear refutation. Yet it now seems to me that if Black follows up with 18...Ne4! 19 Ne4 (19 Be4 Qd3!)19...Qh4 (not 19...Bd5?! as 20 0-0 Be4 21 Ba2 Bg6 22 Bb2 leaves Black without full equality) 20 Kd1 Re4 21 Be4 Qe4 **(Diagram 48)** then things are not quite clear. True, at the moment he has just three pawns for his rook, but White cannot stop him winning a fourth, and then, with his sound structure and the white king still far from secure, it could be that Black's chances are none the worse?! At any rate, I for one would be prepared to play Black there.

d2) 16...dc3 17 e4 Re8 (not 17...Qd4 as 18 Nf5! Qe5 19 Bf4 Qe6 20 Qc3 wins, e.g. 20...Rfe8 21 g4!). 18 Bg5? would lead to a harvest of the white pieces after 18...Ne4! 19 Bd8 Ng3, but 18 Qc3 transposes to d12).

d3) 16...de3!? Black just opens the e-file. After 17 Be3 Re8 he certainly has compensation.

16...Re8

Now, however, White's game is probably beyond saving.

17 Nf5

Having taken just a couple of minutes to make his previous move, Lev thought for over an hour on this one. He explained that his first idea had been to continue with 17 Kf2 Ng4 18 Kg1 until he spotted 18...Qd4! Black's big threat is then 17...Qd4 and this is very hard to meet. 17 Ne4 loses to 17...Ne4 18 Be4 Qh4.

17 Ne2 may be met by 17...Be2 18 Ke2 Qd4 when 19 Qa8 Qa1 wins for Black and both 19 Ra2 or 19 Bd2 are strongly answered by 19...Nd5 (20 Qa8 Qg4).17 Ba2 Qd4 18 Bc4 Qc4! leaves the white king still stuck in the centre. 19 Kf2 loses to 19...Ng4 20 Kg1 Qc3, so 19 Bd2 looks best but then 19...Rad8 gives Black wonderful play for his slight material investment, as shown by such variations as 20 Qf3 Ng4 21 Qe2 Re3!

17...g6!

Straightforward. If the knight goes back 18...Qd4 decides. 18 Nd6 loses to 18...Bd5 and 18 Nh6 leaves the knight stranded after 18...Kg7.

18 Ba2

Ingenious, but insufficient.

18...gf5! 19 Bc4 Qd4 20 0-0 Qa1 21 g4

I had anticipated 21 Qb7, but Lev said that he regarded 21 g4 as his last chance.

21...Ng4 22 h3 Qc3! 23 Bf7 Kf7 24 hg4 Rad8 25 Qh6

In severe time pressure. 25 Rf5 Kg8 26 Rg5 Kh8 was also hopeless.

25...Kg8 26 gf5 Qg7 0-1

Chapter Three

Isolated Queen Pawn Attacks

Russian-Irish GM Alexander Baburin wrote a book about the middlegame with the isolated queen pawn, and I heartily recommend studying it. Opinions on the IQP vary, even at the highest levels. I once heard Seirawan explaining that it was not the IQP so much which constituted a problem, rather the weakness of the square in front of it.

Larsen says that when playing against an IQP your aim should not be to blockade it but simply to win it!

Robert Byrne said that, in his youth, he had considered the IQP a hopeless weakness, but study of the games of the all-rounder Boris Spassky had caused him to see the dynamic potential it can yield a gifted attacker.

Broadly speaking, the fewer the number of pieces, the more of a headache the IQP tends to become. But with more firepower in play it may generate just the kind of middlegame an attacking player seeks. Additionally (with the standard d4-pawn, for example) the squares e5 and, less frequently, c5 (or e4 and c4 for Black) present outposts for knights from where they may often operate with great effect.

The minor piece incendiaries I lob kingward in the opening game of this chapter are maybe no more than *aggressive* moves, for Black had little trouble in repelling the attack.

But note that they did succeed in removing important parts of the defending king's cover. And when he unwisely allowed me a second wave, it was that factor which proved decisive.

Game 18
□ **Plaskett** ■ **Lobron**
EEC Championship, Paris 1983

I won this event with 8/9, thus making my first GM norm with an extra point. The only one other occasion when I recorded a result of over 2720 was when winning the British Championship in 1990. It's tough at the top.

1 d4 d5 2 Nf3 e6 3 Bf4 Nf6 4 e3 Nbd7 5 c4 Bb4! 6 Nc3 c5! (Diagram 1)

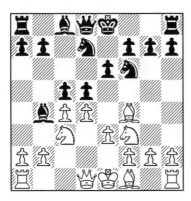

Diagram 1
An equalising blow

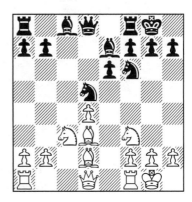

Diagram 2
A typical IQP

In the Ragozin Defence to the Queens Gambit White's bishop now stands on g5. Eric commented afterwards that to play as he does with it on f4 ought to be a very effective method, and I agree. However, I noticed him yawning during the game. Paris has its attractions for a young man.

7 Bd3 cd4 8 ed4 dc4

To have castled immediately would have granted White an edge after 9 c5.

9 Bc4 Nb6 10 Bd3

Perhaps 10 Bb3 is preferable.

10...Nbd5 11 Bd2 0-0 12 0-0 Be7 (Diagram 2)

Black has played the opening excellently.

13 Bg5 b6

13...h6 is also fine.

14 Ne5 Bb7 15 Qf3

In all three of my attacks in this section my queen swiftly made its way to the kingside.

15...Rc8 16 Rfe1

Now I am pretty much mobilised but I have not achieved much, and here Black could have equalised comfortably with 16...Nd7.

16...Ne8 (Diagram 3)

Another logical move, although it does present White with an unusual complicating possibility.

17 Bh7!

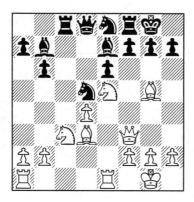

Diagram 3
White has an attacking idea

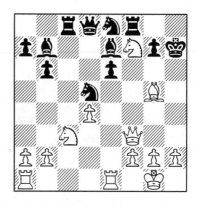

Diagram 4
A complex position

I duly took the option. The text certainly ought not to win but it keeps equality more and less in hand and it does succeed in complicating matters. I now feel that the move deserves the '!' – not so much, perhaps, because it leads to any objective advantage, but for the alternative reason; namely that all alternatives may well leave me simply worse off with my IQP and with insufficient compensatory activity!

Perhaps my captures at h7 and (soon) f7 in this game were attacking gestures, or perhaps they were just a means with which to get myself out of positional trouble?! But they did serve to keep the game going, and in a setting where my chances are by no means clearly the worse.

17...Kh7 18 Nf7 (Diagram 4) 18...Rf7!

There are four other principle 'candidate moves' available.

a) 18...Qd7?! 19 Qh3 Kg8 20 Ne5 Qd6 21 Ne4 and Black must let e6 fall with disastrous consequences. It was this variation which first prompted me to take 17 Bh7 seriously.

Alternatively, 20...Rc3 21 bc3 Qd6 22 Be7 Ne7 23 Nc4 and e6 falls and White has a rook and three pawns against the two minor pieces.

b) 18...Kg8?! 19 Nd8 Rf3 20 Be7 and Black will not achieve equality, e.g. 20...Ne7 21 Nb7 Rfc3 (21...Rf6 22 Ne4 rescues the knight) 22 bc3 Rb8 23 Re6 Rb7 24 Rae1 Kf7 25 c4 etc.

c) 18...Bg5?! 19 Qe4 g6 20 Nd8 and Black is short of equality.

d) 18...Qc7!? is interesting. I did not consider this move at all but it seems quite viable, with perhaps 19 Qh3 Kg8 20 Ne5 Bg5 21 Qe6 Kh7 22 Qg6 or 22 Nd5 being the most rational continuations. I don't think play would be clear in either case.

19 Qf7 Bg5 20 Qb7 Nd6 21 Qa6

Definitely not 21 Qa7?? Ra8 etc.

21...Nc3 22 bc3 Rc3 23 Re6 Qc8! 24 Qe2 Qc4 25 Qe5 Bf4??

A thoroughly irrational move. Correct, of course, was 25...Rc1 26 Rc1 Qc1 27 Qe1 Qe1 28 Re1, when 28...Bd2! leaves things about level.

26 Qh5 Bh6 27 Qg6 Kh8 28 g3

Black is completely busted: his pieces completely lack co-ordination.

28...Rc1 29 Rc1 Qc1 30 Kg2 Qc6 31 f3 1-0

The checks come to an end, and so does the game.

Unfortunately for Black in the following game his 12th move is an outright blunder but, as I was to discover later, it is known to have occurred at least twice before in GM praxis!

Game 19
□ **Plaskett** ■ **Arkell**
Watson, Farley & Williams, London 1991

1 Nf3 Nf6 2 d4 e6 3 e3 c5 4 Bd3 b6 5 0-0 Be7 6 c4 Be7 7 Nc3 cd4 8 ed4 d5 9 cd5 Nd5 10 Ne5!? (Diagram 5)

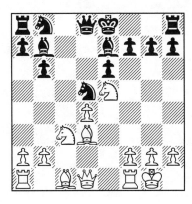
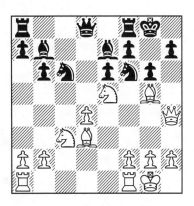

Diagram 5	**Diagram 6**
Probing...	White has a surprising win

This exploratory move had been tried before with success.

10...0-0 11 Qg4!? Nf6

11...f5 might be worth a go.

12 Qh4 Nc6?? 13 Bg5 g6 (Diagram 6)

13...h6 14 Bf6 Bf6 15 Qe4 and White wins easily.

14 Ba6!

Since capturing this bishop allows 15 Nc6 and the knocking out of all Black's props, Black is finished.

14...h6

There is nothing better. Arkell wriggles as best he can, but his cause is already beyond saving.

15 Bh6 Nd5 16 Qh3

This retreat enables White to maintain all the juicy tactics.

16...Nc3

16...Ba6 17 Nc6 Qd6 18 Nd5 ed5 19 Ne7 Qe7 20 Bf8 and White wins.

17 Bb7 Ne2 18 Kh1 Ncd4 19 Bf8 Bf8 20 Ba8 Qa8 21 Qe3 Qd5 22 Rae1 Bd6 23 f4 g5 24 Re2 1-0

Game 20
☐ **Plaskett** ■ **Short**
British League, Birmingham 2000

---

1 e4 e6 2 d4 d5 3 Nd2 Be7

Favoured previously by Joksic and Romanishin.

4 Ngf3 Nf6 5 Bd3 c5 6 c3?! (Diagram 7)

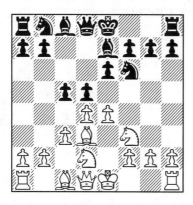
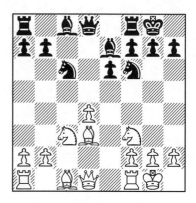

Diagram 7	Diagram 8
Rather insipid	White has lost a tempo

I played this quite a bit around the time of this game. It's not good.

6...Nc6 7 0-0?

And this move should really be classified not just as inferior but as an outright error, for now White will not be able to challenge for an opening advantage. With 7 e5 Nd7 8 0-0 we would have entered a line where White frequently sacrifices a central pawn for the initiative. Despite past successes in the hands of accomplished attackers such as Keres and Nunn, its reputation fell under something of a cloud when, in the 1980s and 1990s, disobliging handlers of the black pieces took to preferring non-acceptance of White's gambit and instead started flicking in ...g7-g5 around moves 8-10. This is now regarded as the best treatment.

7...de4

7...0-0?! 8 e5 leads to a line where White can certainly hope to be better, and it featured in a theoretical article by Nunn in 1978. Short's move ensures I will come out of the opening with zilch.

8 Ne4 cd4 9 cd4 0-0 10 Nc3 (Diagram 8)

As an illustration of the worthlessness of my c2-c3 idea, consider that this position is well known to theory – it's even been dubbed 'The Isolated Queen's Pawn Position' – and may arise from a number of different openings, including the Panov-Botvinnik Attack and some queen's pawn systems. But in all of these it is *White* to move! Consequently 10 Ng3 or 10 Be3 might be tried here, but Black ought to be happy with the opening.

10...b6 11 Re1 Nb4

11...Bb7 is also healthy.

12 Bb1 Bb7 13 Ne5 Nbd5?!

13...Nc6 would have left White with nothing at all, and 13...Rc8 is also better than the text. Short later wrote that he appreciated that his choices hereabouts were inferior even whilst he was playing them. Curious.

14 Qd3 Rc8 15 Qh3

Baburin points out that this is often an ideal attacking post for the queen in IQP positions, many of which, naturally, stem from queen's pawn openings. Indeed this very game cropped up in a book of Gary Lane's on the Colle system.

15...Nc3 16 bc3 Qd5

Threatening to overload White's queen with 17...Rc3.

17 Bd2 (Diagram 9)

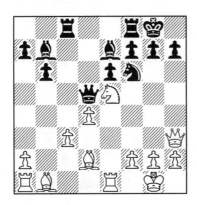

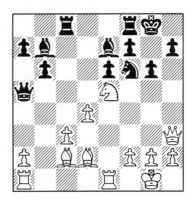

Diagram 9
All been seen before

Diagram 10
What is the best way forward?

17...g6?

To my astonishment I was later to discover that not only is this position known to theory but that the previous occurrence was even in a tournament in which I competed!

J.Kristiansen–Hansen, Esbjerg 1985 continued 17...b5!, which was also a post mortem suggestion of Speelman's. That game had actually begun as 1 e4 c5 2 c3 (!).

After the text, Black's second inaccuracy, Short's game is already critical.

18 Bc2 Qa5 (Diagram 10)

Out of harm's way, perhaps, but this is a remote posting.

19 Qh4?

After 49 minutes' thought I produced an inferior move, which has ideas associated with pressure through Bg5. But even in the game Black easily dealt with that problem with ...Nd5.

It was correct to shift the bishop to a more potent diagonal with the simpler 19 Bb3!, after which Black would be in serious trouble, as the following variations demonstrate:

a) 19...Bd5 20 Qh6 (protecting d2 and so threatening 21 c4) 20...Ne4 21 Re4! Be4 22 Re1 and as Re3-h3 follows, the attack triumphs.

b) 19...Nd5 20 Qh6 Qa3 21 Bd5! Bd5 22 Re3 Qb2 and White might even have 23 Rh3! Qa1 24 Bc1 as Black must now play 24...Qc1 25 Qc1 and White is still attacking. Or 20...Rfd8 21 c4 Bb4 22 Bb4 Nb4 23 Re3 and the attack works.

c) 19...Ne4 20 Be6! and White will win after either 20...fe6 21 Qe6 Kh8 22 Qe7 or 20...Nd2 21 Nf7! etc.

19...Rc3?

Played very quickly, but I am sure that this exchange offer was not the right way to benefit from white's inaccurate 19th move. 19...Rc7! keeps the rook both active and with lateral defensive potential.

20 Bb3

White is in no hurry to capture the rook, instead giving the bishop a new agenda.

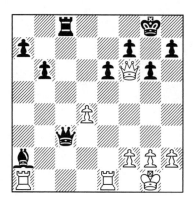

Diagram 11
... Ba2 – a strange tactic

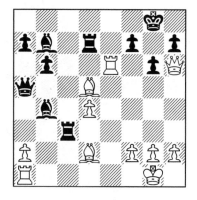

Diagram 12
A curious symmetry

20...Nd5 21 Qh6 Bb4?

Perhaps Black had already entertained this idea when taking on c3, but it drags one piece too many away from his king. I quickly spotted the refutation. I had been concentrating on a defence based upon keeping the important bishop closer to the action zone, starting with 21...Bf6, when play can continue 22 Nd7 Bg7 23 Qh4 Rfc8 24 Bc3 (finally) 24...Qc3 25 Bd5 Bd5 26 Nf6 Bf6 27 Qf6. But afterwards Morozevich pointed out that here Black has 27...Ba2! (**Diagram 11**)

And the fight continues...

22 Nd7! Rd8 23 Bd5 Rd7

Forced due to the threat of 24 Nf6. I guess he had planned on 24 Bb7 Rb7 25 Bc3 Bc3 26 Rac1 Rb8 with reasonable compensation.

24 Re6! (Diagram 12)

Black's body language suggested that this came as a surprise.

24...fe6

24...Bf8 25 Qf8! mates. 24...Rc8 was the most demanding defence, when the newly penetrated rook must switch to a lateral role: 25 Rg6! hg6 26 Qg6 Kh8 and White will pick off the loose rook on d7 with circling checks, e.g. 27 Qh5 Kg8 28 Qg4 and wins.

Alternatively if Black runs we may hunt him down, even minus a rook: 26...Kf8 27 Bh6 Ke8 28 Qg8 Ke7 29 Qf7 Kd6 30 Bf4 mate, or 30...Kd8 31 Bg5 and he can run but he cannot hide, e.g. 31...Kc7 32 Rc1 Kb8 33 Bf4, or 32...Bc3 33 Bf4 Kd8 34 Qf8 mate.

25 Be6 Kh8 26 Bc3 Rd8 27 Qf4 1-0

27...Rf8 28 d5! heralds mate.

In our next game we see a transfer of a white rook from e1, up to e3 and then across to take aim at the black king. This is an important motif, and one which I first saw used by Keene to defeat Miles at Hastings in 1976.

Game 21
□ **Plaskett** ■ **Knott**
Hastings 1999

---

1 e4 e6 2 d4 d5 3 Nd2 Nf6 4 Bd3 c5 5 c3 Nc6 6 Ngf3 cd4 7 cd4

Miles once said that he tried to come up with surprise opening weapons which were good for about twenty games. This c3 idea is now spent.

7...Nb4 8 Bb1 de4 9 Ne4 Be7 10 0-0 0-0 11 Re1 Bd7 (Diagram 13)

Perhaps this is a new move.

12 Nc3

White has taken too long to get his knight to this square, but Black handles the early middlegame inaccurately and drifts into too passive a position.

12...Bc6

This is the way they used to fianchetto in bygone days.

13 Ne5 Rc8

In reply to 13...Nbd5 I would have played the familiar 14 Qd3.

14 Re3!? (Diagram 14)

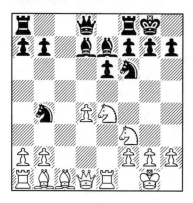
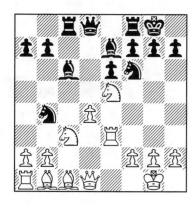

Diagram 13
An unusual development

Diagram 14
A swinger

The rook lift.

14...Nbd5 15 Rh3

In 1976 Keene positioned his rook on g3 and used it as a cannon to blow up the fortress at g6 (with the aid of sacrifices of a knight and a bishop on that square and then, when all was rubble, the final detail of Qb1! for the final, decisive introduction of the queen).

Here too, placement at g3 was to be seriously considered.

15...Nc3

Again we see this transformation of the pawn structure. Now d4 is no longer weak, but the new c-pawn could be.

16 bc3 Be4?!

This misfires because Black trades off a dangerous attacker but allows the white queen to find a powerful. Active defence with 16...Qd5 was certainly better.

17 Be4 Ne4 18 Qh5 Nf6 19 Qh4 (Diagram 15)

The queen looks menacing teamed up with the rook.

19...Qa5 20 Bd2 Qb5

Now I calculated that I could go for victory, notwithstanding any mischief he might wreak against my queenside.

21 Bg5 Qb2 22 Rc1

White tries to tread a fine line between the prosecution of the attack and dealing with the opposition's attempts at counterplay.

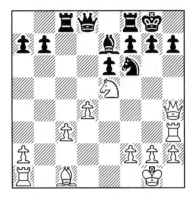

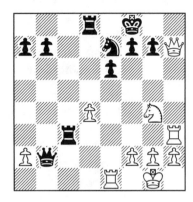

Diagram 15
Menacing

Diagram 16
White has broken through

TIP: It often pays to find a balance when attacking in order to deny the opponent useful counterplay.

22...Rfd8 23 Ng4

Now I start the hand-to-hand combat.

23...Kf8

Black craftily exploits the need for my bishop to defend c1.

24 Re1

White addresses the implication of ...Kf8, and I also bring my rook to a more active square.

24...Ng8

A retreat that is no doubt induced by the pressure Black is experiencing.

25 Be7 Ne7 26 Qh7

After a patient but determined build-up White makes significant inroads.

26...Rc3 (Diagram 16)

Too little, too late.

27 Qh8!

Vacating h7 for the rook.

27...Ng8 28 Rh7

The decisive incursion – g7 falls and with it any hope of defence.

28...Ke7 29 Qg7 Rf8 30 d5!

Thanks to the location of the rook on e1 the IQP takes on an important role.

30...Qd2 31 d6! 1-0

Taking the cheeky pawn allows the capture of one of the rooks, while after 31...Kd7 32 Ne5 the f8-rook drops with check.

Note how I had to keep an eye on what my opponent was doing while I attacked.

WARNING: Always consider your opponent's own aggressive possibilities when conducting an attack.

We also saw another vindication in this game of Kasparov's dictum that pawns are important attacking units, the 'weakling isolani' advancing at the end to become my fifth attacking piece, and to finish the whole process off.

There are instances where the advance of the IQP leads to pawn exchanges and in turn an advantageous or even decisive cleansing of the central lines, as shown in the following game.

Game 22
□ **Plaskett** ■ **Edwards**
Hastings 1999

---

1 e4 c6 2 d4 d5 3 ed5 cd5 4 c4 Nf6 5 Nc3 e6 6 Nf3 Be7 7 Bd3

7 cd5 is more theoretical.

7...0-0 8 0-0 dc4 9 Bc4 Nc6

10...b6 11 d5! is uncomfortable for Black.

10 a3 b6 11 Qd3 (Diagram 17)

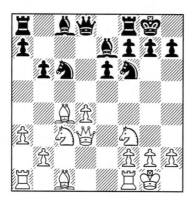

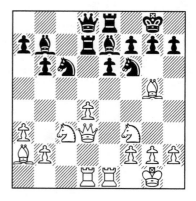

Diagram 17
A typical IQP

Diagram 18
Time for a breakthrough

I first noted the queen being developed on this square in an isolated queen pawn position in a game from a match of 1976, when Larsen used such a deployment to beat Andersson.

11... Bb7 12 Re1 Rc8 13 Ba2

Tucking the bishop away. Instead 13 Bg5 allows 13...Na5 14 Ba2 Bf3, but there too 15 gf3 might be a legitimate try for an advantage.

13...Rc7 14 Bg5 Rd7 15 Rad1

Everybody out!

15...Re8? (Diagram 18)

A well-motivated prophylactic move which arises in similar situations but does not work here. 15... Nd5 was absolutely necessary.

16 d5!

Perhaps White is winning after this advance! This release of the kinetic potential in White's game opens up avenues for the long-range units and facilitates their arrival on strong outposts with decisive effect. However, I can understand that Edwards did not appreciate that the text would work, since he did have a lot of pieces covering d5.

16...Nd5

In the case of 16...Na5 White bursts in with 17 Bf6 Bf6 18 de6! Rd3 19 ef7 Kf8 20 fe8Q Re8 21 Re8 Ke8 22 Rd3, while after the alternative recapture 17...gf6 something like 18 Nd4 is crushing.

After 16...ed5 17 Nd5 Black is faced with a killing capture on f6. Then 17...Nd5 would transpose to the game, but he also has 17...Kh8, moving out of range. I had intended to unpin and move the queen to what is often a significant attacking square with 18 Qf5, when there is no defence against the activity and threats of the white pieces, e.g. 18...Ng8 19 Qf7 or 18...Nd5 19 Bd5, when White threatens not only f7 but also 20 Be4, hitting h7 and d7. If here 19...g6 White wins a good pawn with 20 Qf7 because 20...Rf8 may be powerfully met by 21 Bc6! due to the following continuation 21...Rd1 22 Qe7! Re1 23 Ne1 Qe7 24 Be7 Rf7 **(Diagram 19)**

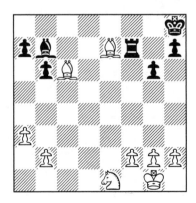

Diagram 19
A zwischenzug is needed

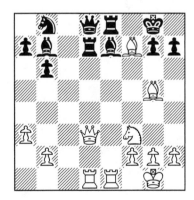

Diagram 20
Splat!

Now 25 Bb7? allows Black to emerge from the skirmish with an exchange after 25...Re7 because of the threats to b7 and e1. However, the neat 25 Bf6! Rf6 26 Bb7 leaves White with two pieces and a pawn for a rook.

17 Nd5 ed5

17...Bg5 18 Nf6 and White wins the d7 rook.

18 Bd5

White now threatens to take on f7 and then d7.

18...Nb8

18...Rd6 does not counter the threat in view of 19 Be7 Re7 20 Bf7! and 21 Qd6. This leaves 18...Bg5 19 Re8 Qe8 20 Ng5 g6 21 Qh3 h5 (21...Rd5 22 Qh7 Kf8 23 Qh8 Ke7 24 Qe8 Ke8 25 Rd5 etc.) 22 Qd7! Qd7 23 Bf7 Qf7 24 Nf7 Kf7 25 Rd7 and the bishop falls.

19 Bf7! (Diagram 20)

Splat!

19...Kf8

19...Kf7 20 Ne5 Kg8 21 Nd7 Bg5 22 Nf6! Bf6 23 Qd8 Rd8 24 Rd8 Bd8 25 Re8 Kf7 26 Rd8 Nc6 27 Rd7 and the bishop falls.

20 Qh7 1-0

Chapter Four

Pawn Rollers

There is a soil amoeba named Dictyostelium discoideum which normally lives a solitary life. Under some conditions, the organisms will voluntarily come together to form a super-organism that is sensitive to light and heat and can move around by undulating like a snake – www.alternativescience.com/alternative-evolution.

'Pawns are the soul of chess' wrote the great Philidor and when they get together, some soulful games may result! As with the soil amoeba the humble pawns may mysteriously link into a greater living thing which has been known to sweep many a strong opponent off the board.

Of all attacking themes, the pawn roller is one of the easiest to grasp, and there are quite a few examples from modern master praxis of a player investing a piece for a clutch of combined and powerful pawns.

Let's have a look at some examples.

In our opener the pawns constitute something of an end in themselves, as they keep going deeper and deeper into enemy territory.

Game 23
□ **Plaskett** ■ **Short**
Banja Luka 1985

A game from a nice Bosnian town, just a few years before it was torn apart.

1 Nf3 Nf6 2 c4 b6 3 g3 c5 4 Bg2 Bb7 5 0-0 e6 6 Nc3 Be7 7 b3 0-0 8 Bb2 a6 (Diagram 1)

9 e3

This approach is too insipid to seriously trouble Black. 9 d4 is best, taking the game into Hedgehog territory.

9...d5

Played after some thought. In our game from the previous year's British Championship he had played 9...Ra7 and, after each of us had declined a draw, he went on to win.

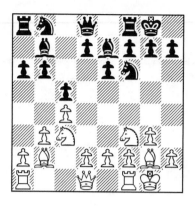

Diagram 1
A quiet opening

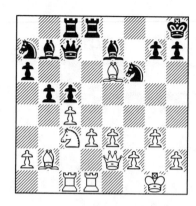

Diagram 2
A latent pawn roller

10 d3 Nbd7

10...Nc6 is more customary, and would have led us into Plaskett-Rogers, British Championship 1988, which continued (by transposition) 11 Qe2 Qc7 12 Rac1 dc4 13 bc4 Rfd8 14 Rfd1 Rac8 15 Bh3!? Na7 16 Ng5!? b5 17 Ne6!? fe6 18 Be6 Kh8 **(Diagram 2)** After 19 e4!? Rb8 20 Nd5 Ian decided to return some material with 20...Rd5 but after 21 cd5 I still had a nasty pawn roller and I won on move 41.

11 Qe2 Qc7 12 Rac1

Played with the notion of having some vague significance in the struggle for the centre, this move soon turned out to have a quite unexpected point.

12...Bc6

12...dc4, as Rogers played, is a more standard way of handling such positions. If White recaptures with the b-pawn Black often, when ...Nc6 has been played, swiftly follows up with ...Na5 in order to render White's c-pawn vulnerable to attack should White play d4.

13 e4 d4? (Diagram 3)

This is a dubious novelty. Although neither of us was aware of it, 13...de4 14 de4 had been played before, when 14...Qb7 is not so bad.

14 Nd5! ed5

Played quite quickly, and with a puzzled and pained expression. 'I just couldn't believe that this was any good.'

15 cd5

Certainly not 15 ed5? Bb7 16 Qe7 Rfe8 17 d6 Qc8 and the queen is trapped.

15...Bb7

Sacrificing back on d5 is not good, e.g. 15...Bd5 16 ed5 Qd6 17 Nd2! etc.

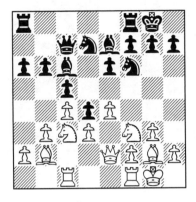

Diagram 3	**Diagram 4**
Retreat the knight?	White's centre is very strong

16 Nd4

Two pawns, the a1-h8 diagonal and the central pawn armada ready to roll looked good to me. But it was only after considerable post mortem analysis that Short's scepticism abated.

16...Rfe8

In reply to 16...g6 I intended 17 Nc2, heading for e3.

17 Nf5 Bf8 (Diagram 4) 18 Ne3

Certainly the right square for this piece, but 18 Qd2 was also strong. It must have been around here that Short appreciated the difficulties posed by my sacrifice, as he thought for 33 minutes before playing his next move.

18...g6

A sensible regrouping. In the event of 18...b5 19 f4 Nb6 we each thought that 20 Bf6 gf6 would be very good for White.

19 f4 Rad8

Black braces himself for the impact.

20 e5 Bg7 (Diagram 5)

20...Nh5 21 g4 allows the effective return of the piece by 21...Nf4 22 Rf4 Ne5, but either 21 Bf3 or 21 d4 leaves White with great pressure.

21 d4!

The key move. The immediate capture on f6 would only have vindicated Black's defence, e.g. 21 ef6? Nf6 and after the subsequent capture on d5 Black will certainly be no worse.

But now White will keep the d5-pawn, and that will make all the difference.

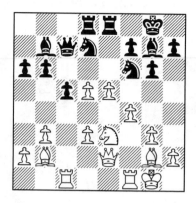

Diagram 5
Should White take the knight?

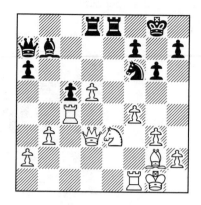

Diagram 6
A useful rook

21...Qb8 22 dc5 bc5 23 ef6 Bf6

23...Nf6 24 Be5 wins for White since the attempt to solve Black's problems with the exchange sacrifice 24...Re5 would be futile.

24 Bf6 Nf6 25 Qd3 Qa7

Now after 26 Kh1 c4! 27 Nc4 Nd5 Black has a lot of activity for one pawn.

26 Rc4! (Diagram 6)

Not only does the rook blockade the c-pawn but it is also a potential attacker because it might switch to the kingside. Of course Black's reply ensures that he may take the exchange – if he so wants – in the near future, but I reasoned that my attack would more than compensate me for the material lost.

26...a5 27 f5!

Commencing the second wave of the attack. 27...Ba6 28 fg6 Bc4 29 bc4 *must* win for White.

27...g5 28 h4 h6?!

28...Ba6 was a tougher defence here because after 29 hg5 Bc4 30 bc4 Qe7! Black resists.

30 Nc4 is stronger, but Black would then have better practical chances than in the game.

Note that 29...Qe7 allows White to wriggle out with 30 gf6 Qe3 31 Qe3 Re3 32 Rg4 and wins.

29 hg5 hg5 30 Qd2 (Diagram 7)

Threatening 30 Ng4 Ng4 31 Qg5.

30...Nh7

30...Ba6 31 Ng4 Nh7 32 Nf6! Nf6 33 Qg5 Kf8 34 Qf6 Bc4 35 d6! Kg8 36 Qg5 and 37 f6 does the trick.

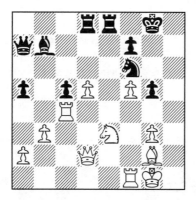

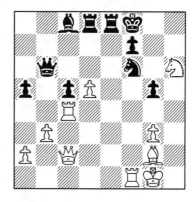

Diagram 7
White's attack begins

Diagram 8
The queen invades

31 Ng4

Threatening 32 Nf6 Nf6 33 Qg5.

31...Qb6 32 f6 Bc8

32...Ba6 would have met with the same end.

33 Nh6 Kf8 34 Qc2 Nf6 (Diagram 8) 35 Qh7! Rd7

35...Nh7 walks into mate on f7.

36 Rf6! Qf6 37 Qg8 1-0

After 37...Ke7 38 Re4 White wins the house.

In the next two examples the pawns steam on specifically towards the enemy king's base.

Game 24
□ **Linker** ■ **Plaskett**
Hastings 1988

1 e4 c5 2 c3 d6!? 3 d4 Nf6 4 Bd3

4 dc5 Nc6!? is an intriguing line.

4...g6 5 Ne2 Bg7

Now we have some form of Modern Defence.

6 f3 0-0 7 Be3 Nc6!?

This gambit offer was inspired by similar ideas in some lines of the Samisch Kings Indian.

8 Nd2

Perhaps White would do better to simply accept the pawn!? I had nothing world-shattering in mind, rather vague ideas of play on the dark squares, with e5 as an outpost for a knight.

8...b6 9 Nf1

This does not look natural.

9...Bb7 10 Qd2 Re8

A standard move in such positions, designed to ensure that White cannot force me to cede my dark-squared bishop after Bh6 (I would then drop back to h8) and thereby worsen my prospects for both attack and defence.

11 g4 (Diagram 9)

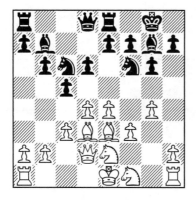

Diagram 9
A central thrust is needed

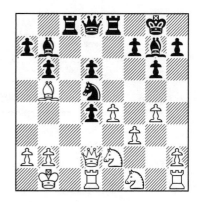

Diagram 10
Where should the knight go?

11...cd4 12 cd4 e5 13 d5 Nd4!

A familiar idea, often seen in the Samisch variation of the Kings Indian Defence. The meek 13...Ne7? would be quite inappropriate here.

14 Bd4 ed4 15 0-0-0 Nd5!? 16 Bb5

On 16 ed5 Bd5 Black will get a third pawn – either f3 or a2 – and an active and reasonable game. Consequently White tries to confuse the issue with a double attack.

16...Rc8 17 Kb1 (Diagram 10) 17...Nc3! 18 bc3 dc3 19 Qc2

Normally the queen's vulnerability to enemy attack makes her the worst of blockaders, but here she will be hard to shift.

19...Re5 20 Ba4 b5

Here comes the roller.

21 Bb3 Qb6 22 Nf4 a5 23 Bd5 (Diagram 11) 25...Ba6

As Gufeld wrote: 'If you are looking for an attack, do not exchange pieces' ... the bishop has a useful attacking potential yet to fulfil, as we shall soon see.

24 Ng3 a4 25 Ka1 b4

Rolling...

26 Rb1 Qa5 27 Rhd1

And now it is time to land.

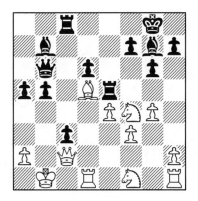

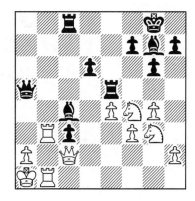

Diagram 11

White's bishop is strong -swop it off?

Diagram 12

How to get the bishops working?

27...b3 28 Bb3 ab3 29 Rb3 Bc4 30 Rdb1 (Diagram 12)

Now capturing the exchange is good enough.

30...Qa2!!

But this is much more fun. 31 Ka2 Ra5 is mate.

31 Qa2 c2

The bishop is fully functional at last! Opening the long diagonal cost me a queen – in order to flush out my opponent's queen – but it was worth it.

32 R3b2

32 Qc2 Ra5 is mate.

32...Ba2 34 Ka2 Rb5! 35 e5

35 Rb5 Ra8 queens my c-pawn.

35...Ra8 mate

In the following game the pawn mass is so effective that it even warrants the investment of a rook.

Game 25
□ **McNab** ■ **Plaskett**
Hastings 1997

1 c4 b6 2 b3 Bb7 3 Bb2 e6 4 Nf3 Nf6 5 e3 d5 6 Be2 Bd6 7 0-0 Nbd7 8 d4 0-0 9 Nbd2 (Diagram 13)

With the knight on c3 and the bishop on d3 we would have a known main line of the Queens Indian, but the way Colin played fails to cause Black any headaches.

9...Ne4 10 Ne4 de4 11 Ne5 f5

Some kingside space might come in useful.

Diagram 13
White is a little passive

Diagram 14
Who will attack on the kingside?

12 Nd7 Qd7 13 f4 Qe7!?

Shifting the queen addresses the possibility of the push c4-c5 and better monitors the kingside.

14 Rf2 c5 (Diagram 14)

Black's latest is not necessary but it seemed to me to be a healthy enough advance. The next few moves contain some very unMcNabish play!

15 g4!? cd4 16 gf5?!

Wild and – ultimately – unsound, the text exposes the king and grants me a monster pawn on d3. However, the play this maverick idea generated, with both bishops and all three major pieces pointing at my king, is indeed dangerous, so I can see why he was tempted.

16...d3 17 Rg2 (Diagram 15)

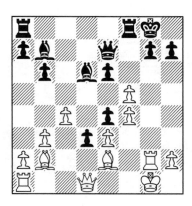

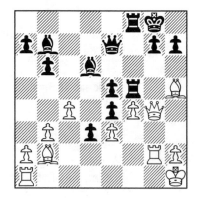

Diagram 15
With some threats

Diagram 16
Can Black defend?

The immediate tactical justification for his idea is that 17...de2 invites 18 Qd6! Qd6 19 Rg7 with a classic windmill discovered check theme. Nevertheless, the long-term drawbacks mentioned in the previous note still apply.

17...e5

This is forced in order to block access to g7 (17...Rf7? 18 Bh5), but it is also a nice move.

18 Bh5 Rf5 19 Qg4 Raf8 20 Kh1 (Diagram 16)

Doctor McNab had correctly foreseen that defence against his straightforward idea of tripling on the g-file was by no means simple here. But he had failed to give serious enough attention to the possibility of counterattack.

20...Rf4!

Defence? Get out of here! However, on a more serious note, I think something is added to the quality of this game if it is appreciated that I pretty much *had* to make this sacrifice.

21 ef4 Rf4

The investment for the three-pawn roller is not, in fact, a rook, but only a piece, as ...e4-e3 will win the pinned rook on g2. Note also that the pawns are already far advanced.

22 Qh3 e3 23 Bg4

23 Qe3 allows the crushing 23...Qg5 with unstoppable threats, e.g. 24 Rg1 Qh5 25 Qd6 Bg2 26 Rg2 Rf1 27 Rg1 Qf3 mate. White now has the defensive idea of blocking the key diagonal by Be6-d5 etc.

23...Bg2 24 Qg2 (Diagram 17)

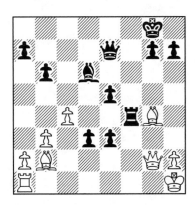

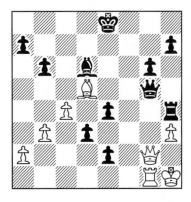

Diagram 17
The tables are turned

Diagram 18
A beautiful finish

24...e4

The pawns roll on, the text introducing the other key player on d6 into the game.

25 Be6

The aforementioned switch, but now the h1-a8 diagonal is not the most important as the h2-b8 diagonal becomes a feature.

25...Kf8 26 Bd5 e2

Simple chess. It is unrealistic to think that such a roller – and do not forget White's less than happy king situation – could be countered.

27 Rg1 g6

Addressed at the threat to g7.

28 Bc1 Rh4 29 h3

29 Bg5 loses after both 29...Rh2 30 Qh2 Bh2 31 Be7 Bg1 and 29...Qg5! 30 Qg5 Rh2 mate.

29...Ke8!?

Can this be put down to learning again from Yusupov's observation on how Gary does it (see the note to move 26 in Game 8) or simply preparation for a sweet finale?

30 Bg5?

30 Bc6 Kf8 31 Bd5 is better, when Black must find an alternative finish such as 31...e3.

30...Qg5! (Diagram 18) 31 Qg5 Rh3 32 Kg2 Rh2 mate

A pure mate: a rare phenomenon in practical play.

Chapter Five

Attacking the Castled King

I repeat: a constant dilemma in attacking situations is whether to employ pawns or pieces. I am not sure that there are hard and fast rules. Reviewing my games, I am left with the impression that I tend to prefer pieces rather than pawns. Pawn rollers, of course, occupy a separate category but, in taking on the kings in this section, in the great majority of instances I seem to have preferred manoeuvring pieces into effective settings rather than smashing through the enemy walls with pawn battering rams.

The castling rule was introduced to speed up the game, and in most modern master games both sides castle. In my opinion, one way of addressing the unhappiness many people have expressed with the extensive analysis of openings might be to modify further the laws of castling. At present one is not allowed to castle if either the king or the rook to be used has moved previously. Why not? Castling is also prohibited if the king is in check or if it would pass through a square under enemy control. Why not?

I would also propose introducing the option of moving the king a little further on. For example, as White, castling kingside currently involves moving the rook from h1 to f1 and the king to g1. But often players will later spend time tucking the king into the corner with Kh1.

I suggest amendments to the laws so that one may, in addition to standard castling, play an 'accelerated' form, in which the king is moved directly to h1. With castling long, there could be an accelerated and also a 'hyper-accelerated' option, with the king moving straight to b1 or a1 respectively. I believe some experimental tournaments with these alterations might be interesting. Just a thought...

Game 26
☐ **Plaskett** ■ **Vincent**
EEC Championship, Paris 1983

1 d4 f5 2 c4 Nf6 3 Nf3 g6 4 g3 Bg7 5 Bg2 0-0 6 0-0 d6 7 Nc3 c6

7...Nc6 8 d5 Ne5!? may not yet be played out.

8 d5 e5 (Diagram 1)

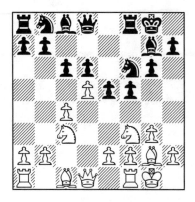

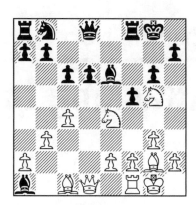

Diagram 1	Diagram 2
Weakening?	With play for the exchange

GM King greets this move with disgust, claiming that it weakens Black too much. Larsen has tried unusual stuff here (8...Bd7!?).

9 de6 Be6 10 b3!?

Offering the exchange which, personally, I would not have accepted.

10...Ne4 11 Ne4 Ba1 12 Nfg5!? (Diagram 2)

A new move, I think.

12...Qd7 13 Nd6

White's activity, development lead, the misplaced bishop in the corner and the slight weakening of the black king (which an ...f7-f5 advance is always liable to constitute) add up to healthy compensation for White's minimal material investment.

13...Rd8 14 Bf4

Defending d6 and attacking a1.

14...Bf6 (Diagram 3)

15 e4!

The best move of the game, opening things up splendidly.

15...Be7

On 15...fe4 16 Nge4 the horses are spinning about Black's camp like whirling dervishes. Meanwhile 15...Bg5 16 Bg5 Qd6 17 Bd8 wins for White, and in reply to 15...Na6 White can splinter Black's structure with something like 16 Ne6 Qe7 17 ef5 gf5 18 Re1 Qd7 19 Qh5 etc.

16 ef5 Bf5 (Diagram 4) 17 Bd5!

Le coup juste, and the full vindication of White's sacrifice.

17...Kg7

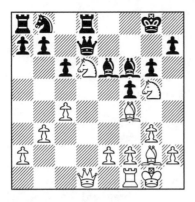

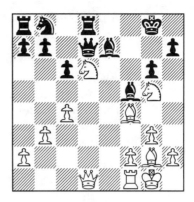

Diagram 3
How to open up the game?

Diagram 4
Spot the tactic

17...cd5 18 Qd5 is a disaster.

18 Be5 Bf6 19 Bf6 Kf6 20 Qd4 1-0

Note that not one of my major pieces has entered enemy territory.

Game 27
□ **Plaskett** ■ **Mestel**
British Championship, Ayr 1978

Mestel and I each tied second in this Championship, won by Speelman.

1 e4 c5 2 Nf3 e6 3 Nc3 Nc6 4 d4 cd4 5 Nd4 d6 (Diagram 5)

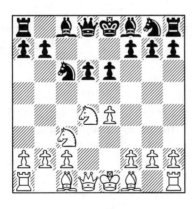

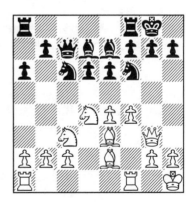

Diagram 5
The Scheveningen

Diagram 6
White prepares to attack

This was unusual for my opponent. Botterill commented afterwards that he felt that Mestel had not really understood this opening. He was certainly never known as an exponent of it. I also noted him yawning several times during the game.

6 Be2 Nf6 7 0-0 Be7 8 Be3 0-0 9 f4 a6 10 Qe1

Modern theory prefers 10 Kh1 here.

10...Qc7 11 Qg3 Bd7 12 Kh1 (Diagram 6) 12...Kh8

Even today I find this a difficult move to rationalise, although it was not unknown then, having been used even by Portisch. One idea is to the avoid problems with e4-e5 which arise in lines such as 12...b5 13 e5 de5 14 fe5 Qe5 15 Nc6 Qg3 16 Ne7 *check*.

13 Nf3

White plans to push with e4-e5. Even I gave this a try with Black, Kosten-Plaskett, British Championship 1986, Southampton, continuing 13 Rad1 b5 14 a3, and Black developed a sufficiently active and viable middlegame with 14...b4 15 ab4 Nb4 16 e5 Nfd5 17 Nd5 Nd5 18 Bc1 **(Diagram 7)**

Diagram 7
Black is solid

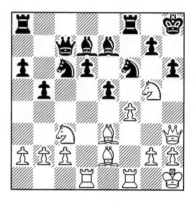

Diagram 8
Black is less solid

The game continued 18...de5 19 fe5 Bb5! (as per usual, exchanges often help a cramped position) 20 Nb5 ab5 21 c3 b4 22 c4 Nb6 23 Bf4 Nd7 24 Bd3 Nc5 (the knight reaches its best square) 25 Bb1 Rad8 26 Qh3 g6 (the only move) 27 Rde1 Rfe8 (preparing the standard regrouping; White's attack is not going to score) 28 Bh6 Bf8 29 Bg5 Rd4 30 Bf6 Bg7 31 Qh6 Rg8 (forced, but White's pawn weaknesses are now about to tell against him) 32 Rd1 Qd7 33 Bc2 Bf6 34 ef6 b3 35 Rd4 Qd4 36 Bb1 Nd7 37 Qh3 Qc4 38 Bd3 Qd4 and Black won.

13...b5 14 e5 Ne8

Black has also dropped back to g8, as Panno did in a similar position against Tukmakov in 1970.

15 Rad1 f5

Breaking out in this manner is often seen, but sitting tight with a move of the queen's rook, or 15...g6, might have been better. In

David–Plaskett, Mondariz Zonal 2000, White had varied with 15 Bd3 and I tried the conventional 15...f5. This was not a pleasant memory, for after 16 ef6 Nf6 17 Ng5 Nb4 my hope that I would be benefiting from eliminating the potentially dangerous attacker proved unfounded after 18 Bd4 Nd3 19 Qd3 Qc4 20 Qc4 bc4 21 Ne6! Be6 22 Rae1 Bf5 23 Re7 h5 24 Rfe1 Bc2 25 R1e3 (even without queens White's pressure is very strong, and Black has no activity) 25...Kg8 26 Nd5 Rf7 27 Nf6 gf6 28 R7e6 d5 29 Bf6 d4 30 Rg3 Kh7 31 Rg5 d3 32 Rh5 Kg6 33 Rg5 Kh7 34 Bc3 Bd1 35 Re3 1-0.

Perhaps White is just better here!?

16 ef6 Nf6 17 Ng5!

It is time for the king to come into focus.

17... h6

Obvious alternatives are few, but now White's superiority is clear.

18 Qh3 e5 (Diagram 8)

That greatly surprised me, and I would still regard covering e6 with 18...Nd8 as superior. Light square weaknesses now appear and d5 becomes available for White's knight.

19 f5

To make something of such an advantage it is not necessary to play for an attack. But leopards, especially teenage ones, have problems in changing their spots.

19...Rad8 20 Bh5!?

Clearly an attacking move, but 20 Bf3 and 20 Ne6, for example, were also excellent.

20...Kg8

20...hg5 21 Bf7 Nh7 22 Bg6 forces mate. Nor does 20...Nh5 21 Qh5 bring much respite.

21 Bg6

The bishop moves into the heart of the action zone. Now 21...hg5 22 Nd5 is obviously terminal. Although the transfer of the bishop to g6 via h5 could hardly be called profound, I have never seen such a manoeuvre in any other game.

21...Nb4 (Diagram 9)

Black is without genuinely constructive moves.

22 Nh7

While this is by no means a necessary continuation (22 Ne6 Be6 23 fe6 was very strong) it is certainly entertaining.

22...Nh7 23 Bh6 (Diagram 10) 23...Qc4?

Losing instantly. Let's look at the alternatives:

a) 23...gh6? 24 Qh6 and the attackers flood in.

b) 23...Rf6 24 Bh7 Kh7 25 Bg5 Kg8 26 Bf6 Bf6 27 Qg4 and the tactical vulnerability of the loose knight on b4 allows White to continue pressing for an advantage, e.g. 27...Qc4 28 Qc4 bc4 29 Rd6, or 27...e4 28 Qe4 Bc3 29 bc3 Qc3 30 Rd6 Re8 31 Qd4! Qd4 32 Rd4 and White wins by attacking b4 and d7, as he does after 31...Re1 32 Kg1! Rf1 33 Kf1 and the double attack is still there.

c) 23...Rf7 24 Bf7 Kf7 25 Qh5 Kg8 26 Bg7 Kg7 27 Qg4 followed by 28 Qb4 with a clear lead for White, although Black is still in the game.

After the text, however, the party will soon be over.

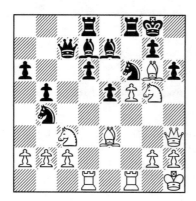

Diagram 9
How to get in?

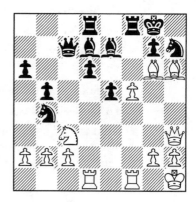

Diagram 10
Black is in great trouble

The critical moment.

24 Bh7 Kh7 25 Bg5

I guess it was this that my opponent had not properly taken into consideration.

25...Kg8 26 Be7 Nc2 27 Bd8 Rd8 28 Nd5 Re8? 29 Nb6 Qc6 30 Nd7 Qd7 31 Qb3 1-0

Game 28
□ Plaskett ■ Short
Plovdiv 1984

I won this tournament and Short came second. This was the critical game.

1 Nf3 Nf6 2 d4 e6 3 c4 b6 4 a3 Bb7 5 Nc3 d5 6 cd5 Nd5 7 Qc2 c5 8 dc5 Bc5 9 Bg5 (Diagram 11)

I think I invented this.

9...f6

9...Be7 10 Nd5 ed5 11 Be7 Qe7 12 e3 0-0 13 Bd3 h6 14 0-0 led to a clear edge for White in Plaskett-Zak, Lewisham 1983. 9...f6 is a slight weakener.

10 Bd2 Nd7 11 e4 Nc3 12 Bc3 Qc8 13 0-0-0!? 0-0 (Diagram 12)

NOTE: Opposite sides castling is often the setting for attacking play from each side.

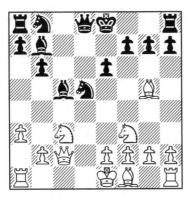

Diagram 11
A new move?

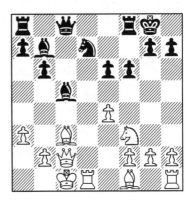

Diagram 12
Who has the safer king?

You will not find many instances of opposite sides castling in the 4 a3 variation of the Queens Indian!

14 b4?!

Speelman commented afterwards that my lack of concern for the safety of my own king in this game was truly wondrous!

14...Be7 15 Qb3 Rf7 16 Bc4 Nf8 17 Nd4 (Diagram 13)

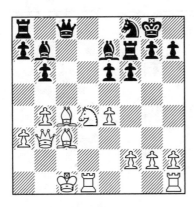

Diagram 13
The e6-pawn is falling

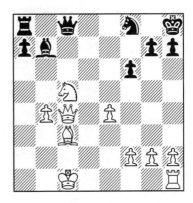

Diagram 14
White's king is airy

Well, my play may have been contrary to accepted rules, I told myself, but, for all that, he is unable to protect e6, so that justifies my eccentricities, does it not?

17...Bb4!

No sir.

18 ab4 Rc7

Luckily, *very* luckily, I have one way out.

19 Ne6 Rc4 20 Nc5! b5 21 Rd4 Kh8 22 Rc4 bc4 23 Qc4 (Diagram 14)

A highly unusual sequence of tactics has left White a pawn up, but with an open king.

23...a5

The tin opener.

24 Rd1

The last piece finally joins the game.

24...ab4 25 Qb4 Bc6 26 Rd6

The longest move, but 26 f3 may have been objectively better.

26...Nd7 27 Ne6

White seems to be going only vaguely forwards!

27...Ra4 28 Qb3 Re4 29 Kd2

An odd move at first glance, perhaps, but the text unpins my bishop.

29...h6 30 f3

An enormous and thoroughly irrational discharge of confidence accompanied the knowledge that I now no longer had to contemplate the arrival of a knight at e4.

30...Ra4 (Diagram 15)

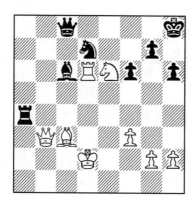

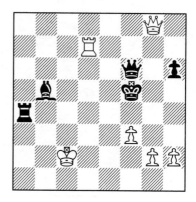

| **Diagram 15** | **Diagram 16** |
| White has a chance | Can you spot the mate? |

This rook is a bit out of play here. White seizes his chance.

31 Ng7!

A shot!

31...Kg7 32 Qe6

Hitting f6 and c6, so Black's reply is forced.

32...Qd8!

Now 33 Rc6 fails to 33...Ne5 34 Rd6 Qd6! – White's drafty king causes him problems.

33 Kc2

There was a slightly superior version of the queen ending that ought now to have arisen after 33 Ke1!? Bb5 34 Bf6 Qf6 35 Rd7 Bd7 36 Qd7 Kf8 37 Qa4 Qe5 38 Kf2 Qh2, although it is still drawn.

33...Bb5

Now 34 Qd5, attempting to exploit the loose pieces, fails to 34...Ra6!

34 Bf6! Qf6 35 Rd7 Kg6??

This loses. Of course he had to take, when after 36 Qd7 Kf8 37 Qa4 White's chain reaction of captures means that he has given up three pieces to win three pieces and a pawn. But with 37...Qg6 Black wins back the g-pawn and has every chance of holding the draw.

36 Qg8 Kf5 (Diagram 16) 37 Rf7

Very practical, but there was mate with 37 Rd5 Kf4 38 Qg3 Ke3 39 Qe1 Be2 40 Qg1 Kf4 41 Qc1.

37...Ke5 38 Rf6 Kf6 39 Qf8 Kg6 40 Qd6 Kg7 41 Qc7 Kf8 42 Qc5 1-0

IM John Hawkesworth went on to become a big Government economist. But he got his calculations wrong in this next game.

Game 29
☐ **Hawkesworth** ■ **Plaskett**
Hastings 1981

---

1 c4 b6 2 Nc3 e6 3 d4 Bb4 4 e3 Bb7

Short and I both now feel that 4...Bc3 is Black's best here.

5 Ne2 f5

And here 5...Nf6, transposing to a line of the Nimzo, might be better.

6 a3 Bd6 7 d5?!

An attempt to drown out the effect of Black's minor pieces through gaining space, but it is not the most effective. Ivan Sokolov played 7 b4! against me at Hastings 16 years later, and it does not look like Black's opening is really working then.

7...Nf6 8 Nd4 0-0!? (Diagram 17)

A gambit idea first played by Miles against Fridrik Olafsson at Las Palmas 1978.

9 g3

In reply to 9 de6 Black anyway plays 9...Ne4!, with active play and a development lead.

9...Ne4! 10 Ne4 fe4 11 de6 Qf6 12 Qe2 Nc6!

Continuing in the gambit vein, although 12...de6 was a possibility.

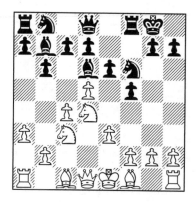

Diagram 17
A gambit

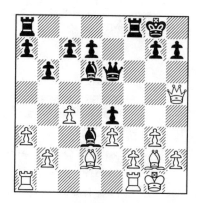

Diagram 18
A huge bishop

13 Nc6 Bc6 14 Bg2

On 14 ed7 there might follow 14...Bd7 15 Bg2 Bg4! and 16...Bf3 with an initiative and compensation.

14...Qe6 15 0-0 Ba4!

A surprising winner!

16 Bd2 Bc2 17 Qh5 Bd3 (Diagram 18)

This bishop rips White's position apart.

18 Rfc1 Rf5 19 Qd1 Raf8!

The loss of the exchange hardly matters. To take the rook White must part with his key defender.

20 Bh3 Qf7 21 Bf5 Qf5 22 Qe1 Qh3 23 Rc3 Rf5

Crude, but devastatingly effective.

TIP: In attacking situations, the most direct moves are often the best.

24 f4 ef3 25 Qf2 Bg3! 0-1

Blasting in – 26 Qg3 meets with 26...f2, while 26 hg3 Rh5 is final.

Grandmaster Chris Ward was British Champion in 1996. He is as good a ballroom dancer as a chess player, and divides his energies between the two talents. More women on the dance floor, though.

Game 30
□ **Ward** ■ **Plaskett**
British Championship 1989, Plymouth

1 d4 Nf6 2 c4 e6 3 Nc3 Bb4 4 g3!?

Alekhine experimented with this, and then in the 1970s so did Romanishin, until it finally became respectable when Kasparov beat Karpov with it twice in 1980s World Championship matches.

4...0-0 5 Bg2 d6

5...d5 is good, with a Catalan flavour.

6 Nf3 b6 7 Qb3 Bc3 8 Qc3 Bb7 9 0-0 Nbd7 10 b3 Qe7

Simpler and superior to 10...a5?!, as in Ubilava-Plaskett, Sochi 1984, although Black went on to win.

11 Bb2 (Diagram 19)

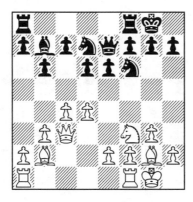

Diagram 19
White has bishops...

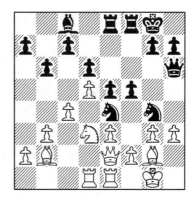

Diagram 20
...but Black has knights!

11...Rae8

11...Be4 is a sound treatment, but less fun.

12 Rad1 Ne4 13 Qc2 f5 14 Ne1 e5 15 d5

The entire plan of closing up the centre has not worked well for White, the edge of the bishop pair now counting for little.

15...Ndf6 15 Nd3 Bc8!?

There is no future on the long diagonal, so White looks for new pastures.

17 e3 Ng4!

Tactically justifiable, and hence strong. White may never get to fork the knights with f2-f3.

18 Qe2 Qg5! 19 Rfe1

On 19 f3 comes 19...Nh2! and White comes out of it badly whichever knight he chooses, e.g. 20 Kh2 Ng3 with 21...Nf1 and 22...e4! most likely to follow, or 20 fe4 Nf1 and 21...fe4 and the g3-pawn's also there for the taking. After 19 h3 Black could sacrifice or just drop back and then soon go to work on the structural concession created by h2-h3.

19...Qh6 20 h3 (Diagram 20) 20...Ng5!

Attack!

21 Qf1

This does not alter things much. After 21 hg4 fg4 Black's aggression, with all of his pieces on threatening posts and the new assets of the open f-file and the g4-pawn, can hardly be countered. Variations would be similar to the game.

21...e4!

Now Black is guaranteed use of f3.

22 hg4 fg4

Capturing on d3 was also very strong, but I was fixated.

23 Nf4 Nf3 24 Bf3 gf3 (Diagram 21)

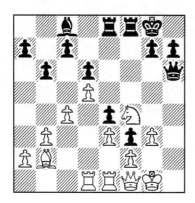

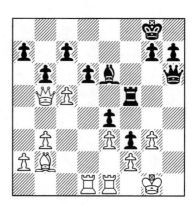

Diagram 21	Diagram 22
Surely this is mate?	An accurate move needed

With this kind of grip on my opponent's bare king a successful mating attack seemed guaranteed to me. Apart from a few last ditch diversions, how can White deal with the imminent arrival of a rook or a bishop on the h-file?

25 Ne6 Re6! 26 de6 Be6

After the latest investment the threat is ...Bh3 to trap the queen, while Black also entertains the idea of Rf5-h5. Black is a rook behind, but so what? White must be finished.

NOTE: Material is just one of many factors in the chess equation.

27 c5

What else?

27...Rf5

Now 27...Bh3?? allows 28 Qc4, and a subsequent 29 Qe4 prepares a defence with Qh4.

28 Qb5 (Diagram 22)

A futile, token hope before resigning. Or so I assumed.

28...Kf8??

28...Qh3 permits White to repeat with 29 Qf1. But I did have 28...c6! when, after 29 Qc6 Qh3 there is no route back to f1 for White's queen. Consequently the search is on for a satisfactory series of checks, but there isn't one: 30 Qe8 Rf8 31 Qe6 Kh8 32 Bg7 Kg7 and the music will soon come to an end.

After the text I believed it was all over, anyway, yet White's position contained just a touch more venom than I had thought!

29 Bg7??

29 Rd4?? does not work in view of 29...Rh5 30 Rf4 Ke7 31 cd6 cd6 32 Qh5 Qh5 and mate on g2 looms. However, there is 29 Rd6! here.

If then 29...Rh5? White mates with 30 Rd8, while after 29...cd6 30 Qc6! it transpires that White has wrought sufficient damage to render a successful finish of Black's attack impossible, e.g. 30...Qh3 31 Qd6 Kf7 32 Qc7 Ke8 33 Qb8 and there's no escaping the checks, or 30...Rh5 31 Qa8 Kf7 32 Qb7 Kg6 33 Qe4 etc. If Black takes time out for 30...Rc5 White may capture with 31 Qe4, when 31...Qh3 is met by 32 Qf3. Meanwhile f3 hangs, and if Black tries to keep it with 31...Bd5 the position remains open and obscure after 32 Qg4.

Sloppy attacking technique on my part, and an illustration of the validity of GM A.Soltis' observation that even poor positions can contain surprising resources.

After my blunder Chris should have drawn this game.

29...Kg7

Normal service was now resumed.

30 Qe8 Rh5 31 Qe7 Bf7 0-1

Game 31
□ **Plaskett** ■ **McNab**
British Championship, 1990 Eastbourne

1 e4 g6 2 d4 d6 3 Nc3 Nf6 4 f4 Bg7 5 Nf3 c5 6 dc5 Qa5 7 Bd3 Qc5 8 Qe2 Bg4 9 Be3 Qa5 10 0-0 0-0 11 h3 (Diagram 23)

11 Qf2!?, as Thipsay once played against me, is an interesting try.

11...Bf3 12 Qf3 Nc6 13 a3 Nd7 14 Bd2 Qb6

14...Qd8!? is also worth investigating.

15 Kh1 Nc5 16 Rab1 Nd3

Knocking out what could be a key attacker, and slightly damaging White's queenside.

17 cd3 f5!

A natural way of holding up White's kingside play. Experience shows that if White is allowed to push f4-f5 in these positions his attack develops very rapidly.

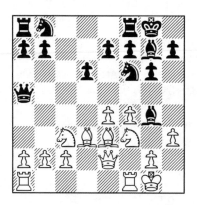

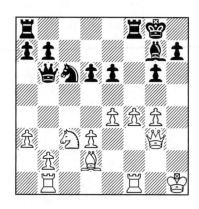

Diagram 23
White has a potential kingside attack

Diagram 24
...Nd4 or ...d5?

18 g4

White continues to bang away.

18...fg4

We have come to a crossroads. 18...e6 is reputable, but I also might have been tempted by McNab's choice as it opens up the play.

19 hg4 e6 20 Qg3 (Diagram 24)

20 Qh3!? is possible.

20...d5?!

20...Nd4 looks better, as in Plaskett-Carr, British Championship 1986. The knight then has a bearing on play in the centre and the kingside. McNab's gambit yields activity for him if it is accepted, but I can decline and carry on my build-up.

21 ed5 ed5 22 f5!

22 Nd5 Qb3 with irritating counterplay. Instead I got on with proceedings on the kingside.

22...Qd8

The queen relocates to where the action is.

23 Rbe1 Qd7 24 Qf3 d4?!

A second unwise advance of the d-pawn, leaving Black in serious trouble. It was better to try 24...Ne5 25 Qd5 Qd5 26 Nd5 Ng4, although even here 27 Bb4 is enough for a slight edge.

25 Ne4 (Diagram 25)

A snug and powerful outpost, and the knight lends considerable – indeed decisive – assistance to the attack.

25...Ne5 26 Qh3

Planning Bg5.

26...gf5 27 gf5

This latest trade means that Black will come under pressure down two files, with the excellently placed knight and the f-pawn battering ram adding weight to the attack.

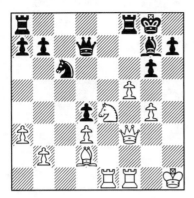

Diagram 25
A good outpost

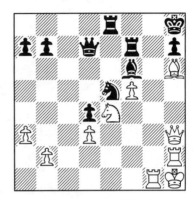

Diagram 26
The build-up is overwhelming

27...Kh8 28 Re2 Rae8 29 Rh2 Bf6 30 Bh6 Rf7 31 Rg1 (Diagram 26)

The attack is about to score, so McNab turns to tricks.

31...Nd3 32 Qd3 Qd5 33 Rhg2! Qf5

Taking twice on e4 walks into mate on g8.

34 Nf6!

Again Black must keep an eye on g8.

34...Qf6 35 Qh3

White now needs only to tidy up.

35...Qc6 36 Kh2 Qd6 37 Kh1 Qc6 38 Qh4 Qd5 39 Qg5 Qf3

Exchanging was, of course, also hopeless.

40 Bg7 Kg8 41 Bf6 Kf8 42 Qg8 mate

Our next instalment is unusual in that the attack features no minor pieces.

Game 32
☐ **Plaskett** ■ **Mestel**
GLC London 1986

1 e4 c5 2 Nf3 d6 3 Bb5

In the previous month I had beaten Mestel with the line 3 d4 cd4 4 Nd4 Nf6 5 Nc3 g6 6 Be3 Bg7 7 f3 0-0 8 Qd2 Nc6 9 g4, but thought it unwise to repeat it here.

3...Bd7 4 Bd7 Qd7 5 0-0 Nf6 6 e5 de5 7 Ne5 Qc8! (Diagram 27)

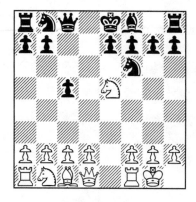

Diagram 27	**Diagram 28**
An unusual queen move	White has the f-file

7...Qc7 8 d4 cd4 9 Bf4 is regarded as better for White.

8 Qe2

GM M.Oratovsky (a.k.a. 'MadMiki' on the Internet Chess Club) is of the opinion that this middlegame is slightly favourable for White. He told me that after he beat me on the white side of it in a Spanish rapid event in 2004. I thought that I had over-pressed, hanging a piece in an equal position.

8...e6 9 b3 Be7 10 Bb2 0-0 11 Na3 Nc6 12 Nc6 Qc6 13 Nc4 Nd7

Black has a comfortable equality.

14 f4 b5 15 Ne5 Ne5 16 fe5 (Diagram 28)

I have the f-file, so maybe I get to attack? Well, a man may dream...

16...c4 17 bc4 bc4 18 Rf4 Rad8!

Threatening 19...Qb6 now that d4 is covered.

19 Bc3 Bb4!? 20 Bb4 Qb6 21 Qf2 Qb4 (Diagram 29)

22 d4!

An unusual exploitation of a lateral pin to secure the d-pawn.

22...Qe7 23 Qe2 c3 24 Qe3 Qa3 25 Qd3 Rd7?!

I prefer a breakout with 25...f5 or 25...f6!? here.

26 Raf1 Rc8

And here I think activity with 26...Qa2 27 Qc3 was more accurate because the passed a-pawn would have been useful.

27 Qf3! Qe7 28 Qh3

After the text White very possibly intends to take on f7.

28...Qg5 29 Qf3 Qg6?

Diagram 29
White has an unusual tactic

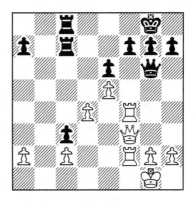

Diagram 30
Time to bring the pawns up

A fundamental error, and probably the cause of Black's defeat. Returning to e7 is best as the queen is rarely a good defender, being susceptible to attack (see Game 24). In fact the queen was far better deployed as a marauder/scavenger on the queenside than at g6.

30 Rf2 Rdc7 (Diagram 30) 31 h4

With White's pieces optimally placed it is time for the pawns! White threatens to prod the queen away from the defence of f7 with h4-h5.

31...Rb8!

Active defence, intending to meet 32 h5 Qg5 33 Rf7? with 33...Rb1 34 Kh2 Qh4.

32 Kh2 h5

Creating a weakness and, therefore, prompting a natural response.

33 g4 hg4 34 Rg4 Qh6 35 Rfg2 Kf8 36 Qg3 (Diagram 31)

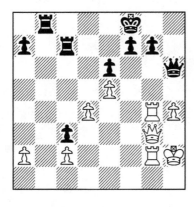

Diagram 31
Black decides to counterattack

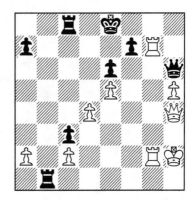

Diagram 32
A final breakthrough is needed

36...Rc4!

Once again Black employs counterattack as his defensive theme, for now 37 Rg7 is met by 37...Rd4 38 Rg8 Ke7 39 Rb8 Rh4 40 Kg1 Qc1 41 Kf2 Rf4 42 Qf4 Qf4 and Black escapes.

37 h5! Rb1 38 Qh4

Threatening mate, and setting up an effective answer to 38...Rc8 in the breakthrough 39 Rg7 Qg7 40 Rg7 Kg7 41 Qf6 Kg8 42 h6 etc.

38...Ke8 39 Rg7 Rc8 (Diagram 32) 40 d5!

A killer of a fortieth move, as an incursion by the queen on the other flank, via Qa4, now becomes possible.

40...Qc1 41 Rg8 Kd7 42 de6 Kc7 and Black resigned.

Afterwards, Jonathan said that he thought he might have been lost for the last twenty moves. This is overly pessimistic, perhaps, but he certainly should have grabbed an earlier chance at counterplay, and 29...Qg6 was definitely wrong.

Game 33
☐ **Plaskett** ■ **Grooten**
World under-26 Team Championships, Graz 1981

I flew via Vienna airport to Graz for the event, where I played the next two games. As I went through the customs barrier in Vienna, a scruffy individual loitering nearby came across and flashed a badge to reveal that he was actually a customs official. As he riffled through my baggage I explained the reason for my visit to his country – 'Ich bin schachspieler' – and he responded 'Ja? Ich auch!' and, now convinced of my integrity, ushered me through.

1 e4 c5 2 Nf3 d6 3 d4 cd4 4 Nd4 Nf6 5 Nc3 e6 6 Bg5 Be7 7 Qd2

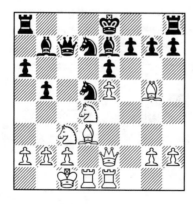
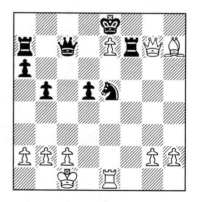

Diagram 33
A sharp position

Diagram 34
Another sharp position

An offbeat system, and probably not very good. A game I played against GM 'Hausigel' in a five minute internet event at Play-chess.com in early 2004 continued 7 f4 a6 8 Bd3 b5 9 Qe2 Bb7 10 0-0-0 Nbd7 12 Rhe1 Qc7 13 e5 de5 14 fe5 Nd5 (**Diagram 33**) 15 Ne6! fe6 16 Qh5 Kf8 17 Nd5 Bd5 18 Be7 Ke7 19 Qg5 Ke8 (19...Kf8 20 Rf1 Kg8 21 Qe7 wins) 20 Qg7 Rf8 21 Bh7 Ra7 22 Rd5! ed5 23 e6 Ne5 24 e7 Rf7 (**Diagram 34**) 25 Bg6! Nd3 (25...Ng6 27 Qg8 and the pawn promotes) 26 Kd2 Qc2 27 Kc2 Ne1 28 Kd2 Re7 29 Qf7 and White soon won. Note the vital role played in this attack by the 'lowly' e-pawn.

7...a6 8 0-0-0 b5 9 Bd3 Bb7 10 f4 (Diagram 35)

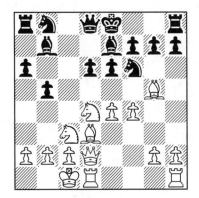

Diagram 35
Can Black take the e-pawn?

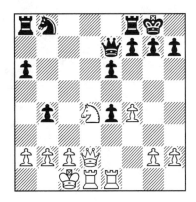

Diagram 36
White has good play

10...b4 11 Nce2 Ne4?!

This treatment does not entirely work.

12 Be4 Be4 13 Be7 Qe7 14 Ng3 d5

In response to 14...Bb7 I would have dropped a knight on f5.

15 Rhe1 0-0

After 15...f5 16 Ne4 de4 White has 17 Ne6!, while in the event of 16...fe4 17 f5 e5 18 Ne6 White wins.

16 Ne4 de4 (Diagram 36) 17 f5! ef5

Or 17...e5 18 Re4 with continuing pressure, e.g. 18...Rd8 19 Qe2! and Black cannot win a piece with 19...Qg5 20 Kb1 ed4? in view of his back rank; meanwhile White dominates.

18 Nf5 Qf6 19 Qd5! Nc6 20 Nd6 (Diagram 37)

Such domination is often the effect of a knight on d6.

20...Ne7 21 Qe4 Ra7 22 Qb4 Qh6

Otherwise Black simply remains a pawn down.

23 Kb1 Qh2 (Diagram 38) 24 Nf5!

A dramatic revelation of the vulnerability of Black's back rank (24...Nf5 25 Qf8! is immediate mate). Hodgson told me that he thought he had seen such a combination before, but could not pinpoint where. Although it is hardly complex, I am not sure that I know of another example.

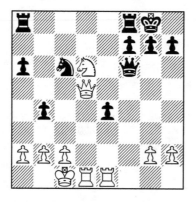

Diagram 37
A dominating knight

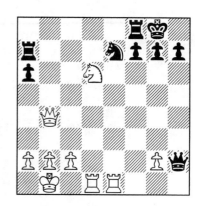

Diagram 38
Loose pieces!

24...Nc6

Losing to a double attack on the loose knight and g7. 24...Ng6 would have lost to another double attack after 25 Qd4. Remember...

TIP: Loose pieces drop off.

25 Qc3 Qg2 26 Rg1 Rd7 27 Qg7 1-0

Game 34
□ **Plaskett** ■ **Braga**
World under-26 Team Championships, Graz 1981

1 e4 c5 2 Nf3 Nc6 3 Bb5

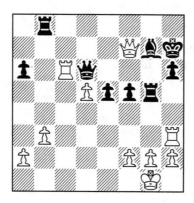

Diagram 39
How to meet 28...Rf8?

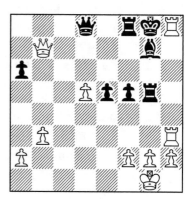

Diagram 40
Mate!

Going into the last round our early lead had evaporated and the Soviets would win. I played Filipovic of Yugoslavia on board three, and the game developed as follows: 3 d4 cd4 4 Nd4 Nf6 5 Nc3 e5 6 Ndb5 d6 7 Bg5 a6 8 Bf6 gf6 9 Na3 b5 10 Nd5 f5 11 Bd3 Be6 12 Qh5 Bg7 13 0-0 f4 14 c4 bc4 15 Bc4 0-0 16 Rac1 Rb8 17 Nf4!? Bc4 18 Rc4 Ne7 (18...Na5 19 Nd5 Nc4 20 Nc4 gives White a monster bind) 19 Nd5 Nd5 20 ed5 f5 21 Rh4 h6 22 Nc4 and I emerged with a clear, healthy extra pawn. There followed 22...Rf6 23 b3 Kh7 24 Rc1 Rg6 25 Rh3 Rg5 26 Qf7 Qf8 27 Nd6! Qd6 28 Rc6 (**Diagram 39**)

I now walked away in confident mood. A spectator gave his approval of my play: 'Yes. Very good endgame.' He was referring to the continuation 28...Rf8 29 Qg7. 'No; better move' was my response. He returned his gaze to the board with a quizzical expression.

When I re-entered the playing hall a few minutes later he was near the entrance and halted me: 'You are a very dangerous tactician!'

Feeling suitably chuffed, I returned to my board, and play went 28...Rf8 29 Qb7!? Rg2. The point, which by now the kibitzer had also spotted, was that if his queen moved to a neutral square such as d8 I had 30 Rch6 Kg8 31 Rh8! (**Diagram 40**) 31...Bh8 32 Qh7 mate. After (29...Rg2) 30 Kg2 Qd5 31 Rf3 Rf6 32 Rb6 Rg6 33 Kh3 Qf3 34 Qf3 Rb6 35 Qf5 Kg8, rather than just winning the game, I simply blundered a pawn with check with 36 a4?? Rb3 37 Kg4 Rb6. Then I tried to break down the fortress, should probably not have succeeded, but did in fact reach a winning position by move 100, only to blunder into a stalemate trap and concede the draw seven moves later. The prize giving ceremony, and even the closing banquet, were long over, when I bumped into the admiring spectator again. This time he only emitted a long, sad 'Ohhhhh...'

Four years later he would become World Champion.

3...e6 4 0-0

Twenty years later 4 Bc6 was the fashion.

4...Nge7 5 b3 Nd4

5...a6 6 Bc6 Nc6 7 Bb2 f6!? was Plaskett-Speelman, Robert Silk Masters, London 1978.

6 Nd4 cd4 7 c3 Qb6 8 Qe2 a6 9 Bc4 Nc6 10 Bb2 Bc5 11 b4!? 0-0 (Diagram 41) 12 a4!?

Incidentally threatening to trap the queen after 13 bc5 Qb2 14 Ra2.

12...dc3

I do not like this move, from which Black emerges with a clear inferiority.

13 dc3

The standard Sicilian pawn structure materialises via a quite unusual route.

13...Be7 14 Nd2 Qc7 15 f4 d6 16 Rae1 Bd7 17 Bd3

White is busy lining up his forces, ready for action.

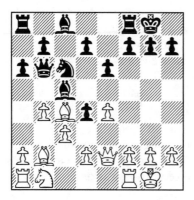

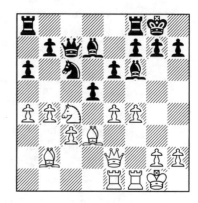

Diagram 41
A strange position

Diagram 42
White has an attack brewing

17... Bf6 18 Nc4 d5 (Diagram 42)

Black finally opts to make a stand by challenging in the centre, but White has an uncompromising response waiting.

19 e5! Be7

Unfortunately for Black White's previous advance sets up the variation 19...dc4 20 Bh7! Kh7 21 Qh5 Kg8 22 ef6, when Black is defenceless, e.g. 22...gf6 23 Qg4 and 24 Rf3, or 22...Qd8 23 fg7 Kg7 24 Qg4 and 25 Rf3.

20 Ne3 g6 21 Kh1

NOTE: So often in attacking games we see the safety of the aggressor's own king high on his list of priorities.

21...f6 22 b5!

After my precautionary measure it is now time to heighten the pressure, the text forcing a useful defender out of play.

22...ab5 23 cb5 Na5 (Diagram 43) 24 f5!

TIP: Capablanca's rule was that if the number of units in the attack outweighs the defence, then the attack should triumph.

There is just too much fire-power pointed at Black's king.

24...gf5

Others get him slaughtered on g6.

25 Bf5! ef5 26 Nd5 Qc5 27 c4! (Diagram 44)

This unlikely advance is in fact the key move of the attack, unleashing as it does a mighty 'extra' piece in the shape of the bishop. The result is that now all of White's forces are engaged in the offensive.

27...Rae8 28 Qh5

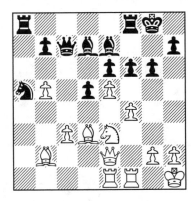

Diagram 43
Breakthrough time

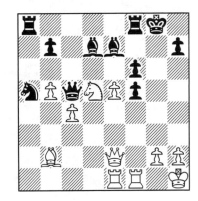

Diagram 44
All White's pieces are working

White has generated threats galore.

28...fe5

28...Nc4 29 ef6 is decisive.

29 Re5 Qc4 30 Rfe1 Bd8 31 Re7! Qf1

We can put this check down to despair.

32 Rf1 Be7 33 Ne7 Re7 34 Qg5 Kf7 35 Ba3 1-0

The next game has the same opening, but this time Black elects to leave his queen at home and, rather than the d-pawn, launches his f-pawn.

Game 35
□ **Plaskett** ■ **Sveshnikov**
Tchigorin Memorial, Sochi 1984

---

1 e4 c5 2 Nf3 Nc6 3 Bb5 e6 4 0-0 Nge7 5 b3 Nd4 6 Nd4 cd4 7 Bb2

This is a novelty (for me!), but clearly at least as rational as 7 c3.

7...Nc6 8 c3 Bc5 9 Qh5!? (Diagram 45)

An interesting, experimental move.

9...dc3?!

Again I do not like this, and would advocate keeping the pawn on d4 with 9...Qb6, as in the previous game.

10 dc3

This is certainly better than a piece recapture and, again, we arrive at the standard Sicilian pawn distribution.

10...Be7 11 Nd2 0-0 12 f4 f5

Since natural continuations like 12...d6 13 Bd3 or 12...d5 13 Kh1 lead to very pleasant positions for White, Sveshnikov, ever the optimist and the would-be aggressor, decided on something more outlandish. Note that the bishop on b5 is now en prise due to the threatened check on b6.

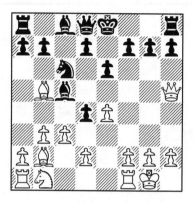

Diagram 45
An experiment

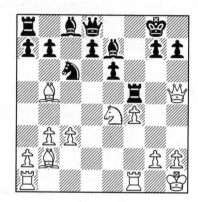

Diagram 46
Draw offer

13 Kh1 fe4

White has a clear advantage after both 13...d5 14 ed5 Qd5 15 Qe2 and 14...ed5 15 Rae1.

14 Ne4 Rf5 (Diagram 46)

This move was accompanied by a draw offer.

15 Qe2 d5 16 Ng3 Rf7 17 c4

Unleashing the queen's bishop and preparing to do some damage to Black's structure.

NOTE: Structural superiority can be a key ingredient in a successful attack.

17...a6 18 cd5 ab5

On 18...ed5 19 Bd3 the d5-pawn is a headache and White's bishops are trained nicely on the enemy king.

19 dc6 bc6

The structure has changed but White continues to be in the driving seat.

20 Rf3

Seeking to activate the rook on the third rank and, in so doing, entertaining thoughts of attack.

20...Bf8 21 Ne4 Rfa7 22 Rd3 Qe8 23 Be5

Simply centralising – and therefore improving – the bishop serves to accentuate White's lead. With this in mind Black now elects to generate some activity of his own.

23...c5

With my opponent endeavouring to get back into the game I reckoned that now – with my forces well placed – was an appropriate point at which to launch a direct strike.

24 Rg3 Kh8 (Diagram 47)

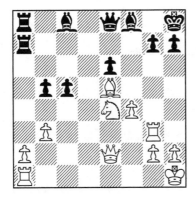

Diagram 47
White has wonderful minor pieces

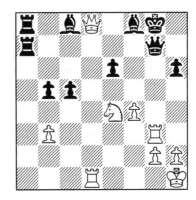

Diagram 48
Black is tangled up

I challenge anyone to locate another Sveshnikov game where, after 24 moves, his most advanced piece was a rook on the second rank!

25 Rd1

Bringing the last team member on to the field. I assumed that the a-pawn would have little significance.

25...Ra2 26 Qg4

26 Qh5? would have been over-exuberant and, after 26...Qh5 27 Bg7 Kg8! 28 Nf6 Kf7 29 Nh5 Be7, White is not winning.

26...R2a7

26...Qg6 meets with 27 Qh4! Qe4 28 Bg7! etc.

27 Nf6?!

A weak move, despite its forcing nature. 27 Rh3! is much stronger, after which I see no way for Black to cope with the threat of 28 Qh4.

27...Qf7 28 Qh4 h6

I expected that 29 Nh5 would now cause g7 to fall and therefore swiftly lead to victory. After 29...Kh7 the sequence 30 Bg7 Bg7 31 Rg7 Qg7 32 Ng7 Rg7 leaves White having to concern himself with the vulnerability of g2, and after 33 Kg1 Bb7 34 g3 Ra2 Black has some counterplay, although 35 Qh5, for example, would win.

However, I have a good attacking position and have invested only one pawn. Unsurprisingly, therefore, I had other good moves.

29 Ne4 Kg8

The return to g8 is forced. Now 30 Nf6 Kf7 leads White nowhere, while 30 Qh6 is met by 30...Qf5! when I saw nothing better for White than 31 Qg6, which was not what I wanted. White has sacrifices on g7 to contemplate, but they do not seem to work: 31 Bg7? Rg7 32 Rg7 Bg7 33 Rd8 Qf8! etc.

30 Bg7!

This is the correct path.

30...Qg7

Black cannot allow the check on d8.

31 Qd8! (Diagram 48)

A good interference move which messes up Black's co-ordination.

31...Qg3

This is as good as any as 31...Rf7 runs into 32 Nf6 Kh8 33 Rg7 Kg7 34 Ne8 and 35 Nc7.

32 hg3 Bb7 33 Qf6 Bd5

More accurate is 33...Be4, although Black is still losing after 34 Qe6 Kh8 35 Qe4 Ra1 36 Ra1 Ra1 37 Kh2. In time trouble, Black now walks into a mate.

34 Qg6

Or 34...Bg7 35 Nf6 followed by 37 Nd5 and White wins.

34...Kh8 35 Nf6 1-0

Commenting on his win as White against Marjanovic from the 1980 Malta Olympiad, Kasparov told me that getting a white knight to f5, in front of a castled black king, may be worth a pawn. Here we see a mirror image example of that precept.

Game 36
□ **Lopez** ■ **Plaskett**
Hastings 1988

1 e4 c5 2 Nf3 e6 3 d4 cd4 4 Nd4 Nc6 5 Nc3 Qc7 6 Be3 a6 7 f4 b5 8 Be2 Bb7 9 Bf3?!

This seems a rather unusual deployment of the bishop.

9...Na5!? 10 Qe2 Nc4 11 0-0-0? (Diagram 49)

11...Nb2!

Thanks to this destructive sacrifice Black is already winning.

12 Kb2 Ba3! 13 Ka3

After 13 Kb3 Qa5 White can stave off mate only at disastrous material cost.

13...Qc3 14 Nb3 Bc6

Threatening 15...b4 mate.

14 Bc5 a5 0-1

Incidentally, the next day, the following position, with Black to play, occurred in a game between Adams and Gelfand in Groningen, Holland: (**Diagram 50**) Boris gained a decisive advantage with the same combination – 1...Nb2!

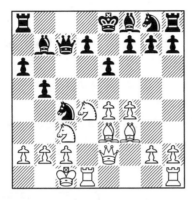

Diagram 49
Is the white king safe?

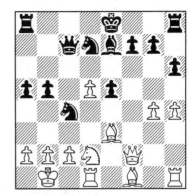

Diagram 50
A similar idea

In 1977 the then World Champion Karpov played a clock simultaneous display in London against ten top juniors. Short, Hodgson and King all lost, as did six others. The one draw was achieved by a boy called Williams. He gave up serious chess not long after that and became an accountant. But 27 years later his younger brother, Simon, would be making GM results.

In our next game the youngster comes under considerable pressure down the h-file after he has castled kingside.

Game 37
☐ **S.Williams** ■ **Plaskett**
London 1999

1 c4 b6 2 Nc3 e6 3 e4 Bb7 4 Bd3

This is a funny, Romanishin-type concept.

4...c5

4...Bb4, 4...Nf6 and 4...f5!? are all alternatives. Hanley – Plaskett, Monarch Assurance Open, Isle of Man 1988, continued 4... Bb4 5 Nf3 (5Nge2!?) 5...Ne7 6 Ne2!? (another exotic move, hoping to show that the bishop on b4 is now out of play) 6...f5 7 Ng3 0-0! (a novelty, and a good one) 8 0-0 (8 a3 Bd6 9 e5 Bc5 10 b4 Bf3 11 Qf3 Bd4 and the bishop counterattacks a rook to escape to freedom) 8...Bd6 9 ef5 Nf5 10 Bf5 ef5 11 Re1 (11 d4 f4, while 11 c5 Bg3!? 12 hg3 Bf3!? 13 Qf3 Nc6 is interesting) 11...Qf6 12 d4 Bf3! 13 Qf3 Nc6 14 d5 Ne5 15 Qc3 f4 (a battering ram) 16 Ne4 Qh4 17 f3 (17 Nd6 Ng4 18 h3 Qf2 19 Kh1 f3! would have won for Black) 17...Bb4!? (17...Nc4 wins but this is more fun) 18 Qb4 Nd3 19 g3 fg3 20 hg3 Qh3 21 Qc3 Rf3! 22 Bf4 (22 Be3 Ne1 and Black wins) 22...Rf8 (winning) 23 Rf1 R8f4! 24 Rf3 Rf3 25

Qd2 Qg4 26 Qe2 Nf4 27 Qe1 Qh3 28 Qd2 Re3 0-1.

5 Nf3 Nc6

Once, in Jersey, I tried 5...g5!? against the same opponent and we drew after a wild struggle.

6 Bc2 Nf6 7 d4

In the case of 7 0-0 both 7...Qb8!? and 7...Bd6!? are interesting replies.

7...cd4 8 Nd4 Qb8!? 9 0-0 h5?!

Black's play is experimental and probably not 100% correct.

10 Nc6! Bc6 11 Qe2 Bc5 12 h3?

But this is quite wrong. Instead 12 Kh1 is enough to leave White with an edge, and 12 Nd5!? is worth investigating.

12...Ng4! (Diagram 51)

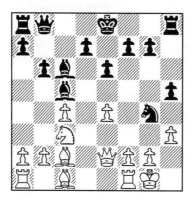

Diagram 51
A dangerous sacrifice

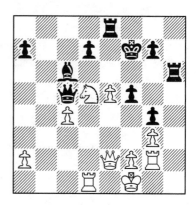

Diagram 52
Black targets the e-pawn

White's last justified my early thrust of the h-pawn and invited this sacrifice, which already secures Black a decisive lead.

13 hg4 hg4

Threatening mate on h2 and therefore forcing White's next.

14 e5 f5!

The key move, exploiting the pin on the h2-b8 diagonal. From f5 the pawn both protects its partner on g4 denies White use of the blockading e4-square. Meanwhile, the transfer of the queen to the h-file is prepared.

15 Bf5

After 15 Bg5 Rh5 16 Qd2 Kf7 Black follows up with the deadly ...Qh8. Consequently this return of the piece is the only way to keep the game going.

15...ef5 16 Nd5 Qd8

The queen edges closer to the h-file.

17 g3 Rh3 18 Kg2 Kf7 19 Be3 Qe7 20 Bc5 Rah8!

Black's mate threats on the h-file outweigh the attack on the queen.

21 Rg1 Qc5 22 Rad1 b5!

A nice, thematic 'weakener' that adds to White's worries surrounding the loose king position, isolated e-pawn and pinned knight by undermining his hold on the centre. In fact White is now under too much pressure across the board.

23 b3 bc4 24 bc4 Rh2 25 Kf1 Re8 26 Rg2 Rh1 27 Rg1 Rh2 28 Rg2 Rh6! (Diagram 52)

The rook finds a more useful role, rounding up the e-pawn.

29 Kg1 Rhe6 30 Rh2 Re5 31 Qd3 Re1 32 Re1 Re1 33 Kg2 Re5 34 Rh4 Bd5 0-1

Game 38
□ **Conquest** ■ **Plaskett**
Hastings 1989

1 d4 d6 2 Nf3 g6 3 c4 Bg7 4 Nc3 Bg4!? 5 e3 Nc6 6 Be2 Nf6 7 b3

GM Conquest has a universal style.

7...0-0 8 Bb2 e5 9 d5

Closing the centre is perhaps not the wisest approach here.

9...Ne7 10 Nd2 Bd7

With such a structure it would be illogical to trade off the light-squared bishop.

11 0-0 Ne8

The standard retreat, preparing kingside expansion with the advance of the f-pawn.

12 b4 f5 13 c5 (Diagram 53)

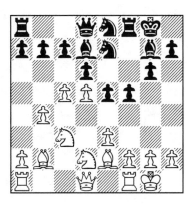

Diagram 53
Typical King's Indian

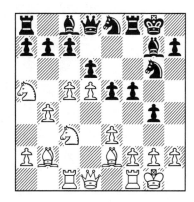

Diagram 54
Black is faster

I once saw Seirawan win a fine strategical game against Ravikumar en route to taking first place in the 1979 World Junior Championship in Skien, Norway, where he also treated the classical Kings Indian Defence in such a manner with the white pieces, adopting a less usual move order by playing e2-e3 rather than the normal e2-e4. That inspired me to give the treatment a go, and I used the concept to defeat Byron Jacobs in 1980 and then lost with it against Erling Mortensen in 1982.

The main line of the Kings Indian is all about timing. The structure confers a space advantage for White on the queenside and Black on the opposite flank. Handled adroitly, theory still regards White's chances as superior, but inaccurate play from White can easily lead him into difficulties.

13...g5

Black launches another pawn in the quest to make my presence felt on the kingside.

14 Nc4 Ng6 15 Na5 Bc8!

Black should avoid making any positional concessions that would help along White's build-up on the queenside.

16 Rc1 g4 (Diagram 54) 17 cd6 cd6 18 Nb5

The c-file is usually White's in this opening but here Conquest's approach is just not working, whilst the storm clouds are gathering fast in front of his king.

18...a6

With the e8-knight covering c7 White must retreat.

19 Nc3 Rf6

A useful rook lift.

20 a4 Nh4 (Diagram 55)

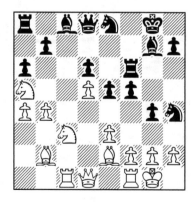
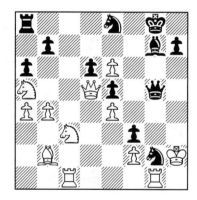

Diagram 55
Storm clouds are gathering

Diagram 56
A plug

Black's increasing share of the territory and looming forces suggest that White's coming defensive task might well prove too difficult.

21 e4 f4! 22 Bg4 Rg6

This is the point behind Black's previous move, the shift to the g-file forcing White to allow entry into his king position.

23 Be6 Be6 24 de6 Rg2 25 Kh1 Qg5

The arrival of the queen after initial progress in the form of a breakthrough tends to signal serious trouble for the defender, and this situation is a typical example. The threat is mate on g2 after a clearing check on h2.

26 Rg1 f3

An important component of the attack – the pawn clamps down on g2.

27 Qd5

There is nothing better.

27...Rh2! 28 Kh2 Ng2 (Diagram 56)

A concept I have never seen mentioned in middlegame texts is that of the plug. We hear about outposts, but not the simple plugging or closing up of a file – often with a knight. In the diagram position the knight on g2 performs this plugging task with decisive effect.

29 e7 Kh8 0-1

Black threatens mate on h4, and if the rook moves away to leave g1 free there comes the deadly 29...Nf4.

Chapter Six

From a Clear Blue Sky

'There are games in chess won by the same style, same manner, same number of moves and even same moves. There are doubles. I think any chess master has his own experience with these doubles' – Lubomir Kavalek.

The determination to play for wins counts for a lot. Nobody ever won a game by agreeing it drawn.

Game 39
□ **Rath** ■ **Plaskett**
Esbjerg 1982

1 Nf3 Nf6 2 c4 b6 3 g3 Bb7 4 Bg2 g6 5 b3 Bg7 6 Bb2 0-0 7 0-0 Na6

Breaking the symmetry, in a known manner. In an interview in 1980, Jan Timman wrote of the difficulty of playing for a win with Black, especially when White only wants a draw.

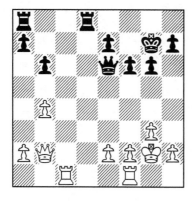

Diagram 1
A quiet position

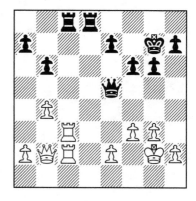

Diagram 2
Black has an idea

8 Nc3 c5 9 Rc1 d5 10 Nd5 Nd5 11 Bg7 Kg7 12 cd5 Qd5 13 d4 Rfd8

This is more accurate than 13...cd4 14 Qd4 Qd4 15 Nd4 Bg2 16 Kg2, when White's superior knight grants him a nagging edge.

14 dc5 Nc5 15 Qc2 Qd6 16 b4 Ne6 17 Qb2 f6 18 Ng5 Bg2 19 Ne6 Qe6 20 Kg2 (Diagram 1) 20...Qe4 21 f3 Qe3 22 Rc3 Qe5 23 Rfc1 Rac8 24 R1c2 (Diagram 2)

White's latest was accompanied by a draw offer. While I was wondering how to spend the free afternoon a very unusual possibility suggested itself. After forty minutes reflection, I decided to try it.

24...Rd1!?

My opponent goggled at the board... and snatched off the rook.

25 Rc8 Qe3 (Diagram 3)

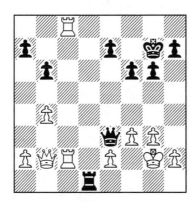

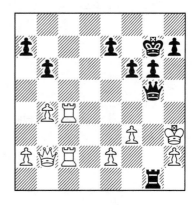

Diagram 3	**Diagram 4**
Not so quiet now	The trap closes

The rook sacrifice is sound. It does not lose, but – against accurate defence – nor should it win.

26 R8c4

Of course we must check out the alternatives.

a) 26 h4?? Rg1 27 Kh3 Rh1 28 Kg2 Qg1 mate, or 28 Kg4 h5 mate.

b) 26 g4?? Rg1 27 Kh3 Qh6 mate.

c) 26 f4?? Rg1 27 Kh3 Qe6 28 Kh4 Qf5 28 Rc5 bc5 29 Rc5 e5 and wins.

d) 26 Qc1? Rc1 27 Rc1 Qe2 and Black will pick off another pawn and stand better in the queen versus two rooks ending.

e) 26 Rc1 Rd2 27 Qd2 (27 Rc2? Qe2 28 Kh3 Qh2 29 Kg4 h5 30 Kf4 e5 31 Ke4 Qe2 mate) 27...Qd2 28 R1c2 Qb4 is roughly equal.

f) 26 Rg8 Kg8 27 Qb3 Qb3 28 ab3 results in an ending where White's rook emerges temporarily poorly placed after 28...Rd4 29 Rc7 Kf7 30 Ra7 Rb4 31 Ra3, although the game should nonetheless be drawn.

g) 26 R2c4 leads to variations similar to the game after 26...Rg1 27 Kh3 Qe6 28 g4 (the only move here).

26...Rg1 27 Kh3 Qe6 28 g4

28 Kh4? loses to 28...Qf5 29 g4 g5 30 Kh3 Qg6 and mate on h6.

28...Qe3!

The only move, threatening mate on h6. Now 29 Qc1 is forced, after which 29...Rc1 30 Rc1 Qe2 31 Kg3 leads to a setting of approximate equality.

But White's unwillingness to part with his ill-gotten gains, plus, perhaps, a sense of disorientation through the unexpected rook sacrifice, were the cause of his defeat...

29 g5?? Qg5 (Diagram 4)

The threats to White's evicted, exposed king are unanswerable.

30 Rg4 Qh5 31 Rh4 Qf5 32 Rg4 h5 33 Rc4 g5! 0-1

Mate with 34...hg and 35...Qh7 is coming, and 34 Qc2 loses to 34...hg4 in view of 35 fg4 Qf1 mate.

Two rounds later, this happened:

Game 40
□ **P.Knudsen** ■ **Plaskett**
Esbjerg 1982

1 Nf3 Nf6 2 c4 b6 3 g3 Bb7 4 Bg2 g6 5 b3 Bg7 6 Bb2 0-0 7 0-0 Na6 8 Nc3 c5 9 Rc1 d5 10 Nd5 Nd5 11 Bg7 Kg7 12 cd5 Qd5 13 d4 Rfd8 14 dc5 Nc5 15 Qc2 Qd6 16 b4 Ne6 17 Qb2 f6 18 Ng5 Bg2 19 Ne6 Qe6 20 Kg2

Here I decided to vary.

20...h5 (Diagram 5)

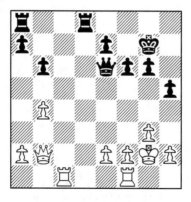

Diagram 5
Another quiet position

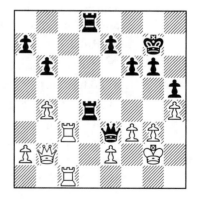

Diagram 6
Black has an initiative

Of course, this should be drawn.

21 h4 Qe4 22 f3 Qe3 23 Rc2

With the interpolation of the rook's pawns' moves the line 23 Rc3 Qe5 24 Rfc1 Rac8 25 R/1c2 Rd1! is even more effective, with, for example, 26 Rc8 Qe3 27 Rg8 now failing to 27...Kh7! and mate.

23...Rd4 24 Rfc1 Rad8 25 Rc3? (Diagram 6)

The beginning of an apparent eviction, but Black's forces will be back with a vengeance!

25...Qe6 26 R1c2?

This abandons the back rank, so dropping the other rook back would be better.

26...Rd1 27 Qb3

White must have thought that with this he had defended himself adequately, but now comes a very nasty tactic that he had overlooked.

27...Qe5!

And now he saw that his intended 28 Re3 fails to the vicious 28...Rg1! and White will be mated. Accordingly, White must now let the opponent's major pieces come flooding in.

28 Kf2

28 f4 Qe4 29 Rf3 R8d2 and Black wins.

28...Rh1 29 f4 Qe4 30 Rf3 Rdd1 31 Rc8

Or 31 Kg2 Rdg1 32 Kf2 Rb1 etc.

31...Rh2 mate

Chapter Seven

Fantasia

I once asked a group of titled players whether the computer is merely a super calculating brain which comes along afterwards to show us where we made tactical oversights, or if we may actually learn anything from computers that is applicable in practical play.

Speelman replied that he thought we could benefit from working with them, and that now 'I sometimes take pawns.'

When working with Kasparov, and seeing how analysing his most interesting games with machines had often revealed startling resources even to him, I was struck by how computer analysis shows us, perhaps more than anything else, how we are limited to patterned thinking. Above all, the 'computer move' is still the unlikely tactical possibility.

In this final chapter I include some games of mine which, in my opinion, featured truly unusual attacking ideas. The material here may be less didactic, but I would hope nevertheless that the games are still enjoyable.

Game 41
☐ **Plaskett** ■ **Hawelko**
European Junior Championship, Groningen 1979

I came third in this event, behind van der Wiel and Dolmatov, but as consolation for only the bronze medal this dear game won me the Brilliancy Prize.

1 e4 g6 2 d4 Bg7 3 Nc3 d6 4 f4 a6 5 Nf3 b5 (Diagram 1)

This is a rare but feasible line which, more recently, has been frequently tried by one of the world's most creative GMs, Tiger Hillarp-Persson.

6 a4

Twenty years later Tiger told me that he considered this to be one of the best moves. However, I am not so sure as White's knight now gets pushed out of the game. 6 Bd3 Bb7 7 a4 b4 8 Ne2 has been recommended, while Adams has preferred (6 Bd3 Bb7) 7 e5!? here.

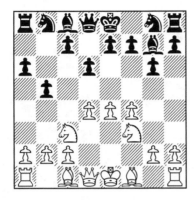

Diagram 1
A rare try

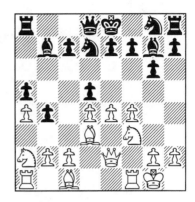

Diagram 2
Black gets it wrong

6...b4 7 Na2 Bb7 8 Bd3 a5

8...c5!? is interesting.

9 0-0 Nd7 10 Qe2 d5? (Diagram 2)

This is definitely wrong.

11 e5

Advancing the pawn gains some useful space and closes out both bishops.

11...e6

Well.... time to attack?

12 g4

I thought so. But these days it would be 12 Be3 with c2-c3 or Nc1 to follow.

12...c5 13 dc5 h5

Black hurries to cause maximum disruption – otherwise he might just get squashed.

14 f5!?

I do not recall spending any time at all analysing the restrained 14 h3.

14...hg4 15 fe6

White ploughs on regardless.

15...gf3 16 Rf3! (Diagram 3)

And here is a good example of improvisation. I had seen that I had at least 16 ed7, regaining the material, but I wanted more. 16 Qf3 Ne5 17 ef7 Kg8 18 fg8Q Kg8 is certainly not a good idea since Black's king has scurried to safety and his forces are well co-ordinated. 16 Qf3 Ne5 17 Bb5 is very good against 17...Kf8?? thanks to 17 Qf7!, but less effective against 17...Ke7. Hence the text.

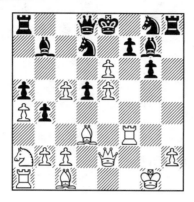

Diagram 3
Better than taking the knight

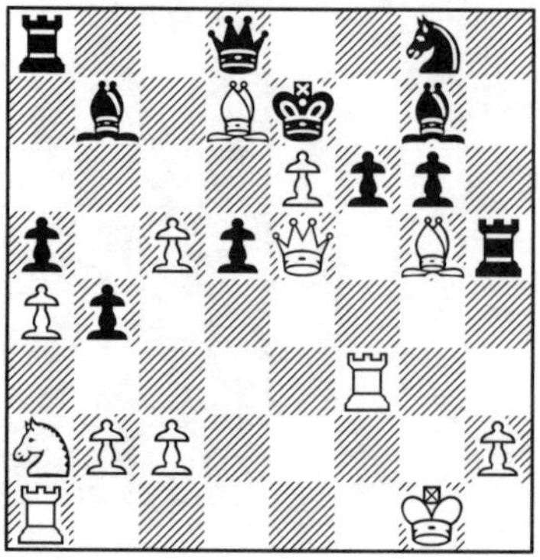

Diagram 4
A highly original move

16...Ne5

The natural move. 16...Nc5 17 Bb5, 16...fe6 17 Bg6 and 16...Be5 17 ed7 followed by 18 Qe5 all win for White. In reply to 16...Qh4 White has 17 ed7 or even the more complex and equally strong 17 ef7.

My original intention had been to meet the text with 17 ef7 Kf8 18 fg8Q, but now after 18...Kg8 I could see chances only for Black. And then there was the check at b5!? It was simple to see that 17...Kf8 loses to 18 Qe5! Be5 19 Rf7 mate, but what about 17...Ke7 here? The point is that after 18 ef7 there comes 18...Ke6!?

Eventually I sighted upon a very unusual tactical idea indeed. I checked the variations, which thrilled me, and then each player made his next three moves immediately.

17 Bb5 Ke7 18 Bg5 f6 19 Qe5 Rh5 20 Bd7! (Diagram 4)

'It becomes more and more difficult to find original combinations in chess, especially in the earlier stages of the game. This, I think, is one of them' – A.Alekhine in his notes to the 17th game of his 1934 match with Bogoljubow.

It was a joy to be able to play such a move. 20...Rg5 21 Qg5 fg5 22 Rf7 mate is the cute point. It should be noted that 20 Re1!? also prevents the double capture on g5 due to the same mate.

20...Ra6

Black guards against the mate on d6. I had expected 20...Qb8 21 Qb8 when White wins after either 21...Rb8 22 Bf4 or 21...Rg5 22 Qg3.

21 Raf1! Qf8

Now 22 Qc7 Rg5 23 Kh1 wins, but I preferred an alternative route.

22 h4!?

A cheeky move. Now Qc7 is indeed coming, and Black is without hope.

22...Rg5 23 hg5 fe5 24 Rf8 Nf6

24...Bf8 25 Rf7 wins for White.

25 ef6 Kf8 26 e7 1-0

Game 42
□ Plaskett ■ Nunn
Borehamwood 1982

Borehamwood is contiguous with the suburb of Elstree. This next game was played within a mile or two of Elstree Studios, where seventeen years later I would twice appear as a contestant on *Who Wants To Be a Millionaire?* Neither was I to prove a winner in either of those two, bigger games.

1 c4 g6 2 Nc3 Bg7 3 Nf3 Nf6 4 e4 d6 5 d4 0-0 6 Be2 Nbd7

6...Nc6 is one of Black's options.

7 0-0 e5 8 d5 Nc5 9 Qc2 a5 10 Bg5 h6 11 Be3 (Diagram 5)

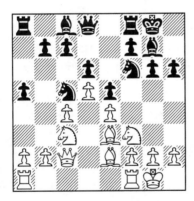

Diagram 5
A standard King's Indian

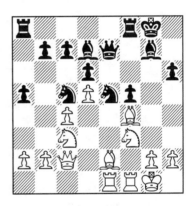

Diagram 6
A new move

Raymond Keene wrote an article about this system in 1978. He dubbed it 'The Proto-Petrosian.'

11...Nfd7

11...Ng4 12 Bc5 dc5 13 h3 Nf6 14 Ne5 Nd5 15 cd5 Be5 17 f4 Bd4 18 Kh2 is a sharper but less trusted line. 11...Nh5 looks rational to me.

12 Nd2 f5 13 ef5 gf5 14 f4 ef4 15 Bf4 Ne5 16 Nf3 Bd7 17 Rae1 Qe7 (Diagram 6)

We discovered afterwards that this was a new move. 17...Ng6 had been advocated, with 17...Qf6 actually being played in two previous games.

18 Ne5

This capture (of an anyway decent piece) establishes a middlegame in which White hopes to target Black's hanging pawns.

18...de5 19 Be3 b6

There now follows some manoeuvring.

20 Kh1 Kh8 21 Qd2 Qd6 22 Bd1!?

White begins a standard redeployment of the bishop.

22...Rf7 23 Bc2 Qf8 24 Ne2

If unimpeded this knight will create problems by landing on h5.

24...Nb7! (Diagram 7)

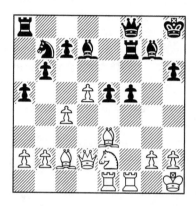 

Diagram 7
Black regroups

Diagram 8
White sacrifices a pawn

An alert regrouping, especially as it involves the retreat of an already well placed piece.

NOTE: Backwards moves of queens and knights are always amongst the most difficult to find.

25 Ng3 is now met by 25...Nd6 (not 25...f4? 25 Qd3 Bf6 26 Nh5 when White is much better), and the genuine threats of the forks on f4 and c4 cut across White's plans. Consequently I took time out to protect the c-pawn.

25 b3 a4

Introducing the possibility of opening the a-file.

26 b4 Nd6

From here on in there is less and less strategical thinking. We have a middlegame with lots of pieces on the board and little in the way of structural signposts for the players, each of whom still had an interest in winning the game. One thing is clear: White's king is the safer.

27 c5 Nc4 28 Qc3 Ne3 29 Qe3 bc 30 bc Ra5!? 31 c6 Bc8 32 Qd2 Rc5!?

Nunn does not like passivity and ventures a pawn sacrifice in order to stay active. After the meek 32...Ra8 I thought that 33 Nc3 would leave White better.

33 Ba4 Qd6 34 Bb3!? (Diagram 8)

This time White invests a pawn for the cause rather than continue 34 Rd1 Ba6 when Black has some compensation. Furthermore, the text is much more fun.

34...Rc6 35 Nc3!

35 dc6 Qd2 36 Bf7 Ba6! 37 Bh5 Qg5 38 Bf7 Qd2 would have been a draw by repetition.

35...Rb6 36 Ne4!

At the time of the game this was considered a real Kasparov move.

36...Qf8 37 d6! Rd7?

Incautious. It was a better practical chance to have tried something like 37...Rb3 38 ab3 fe4 39 Rf7 Qf7 40 Qc2 c5.

38 Qc2! cd6 39 Rf5! (Diagram 9)

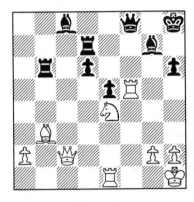

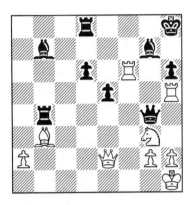

Diagram 9
A crucial pawn goes

Diagram 10
Quite remarkable

39...Qd8!

In the event of 39...Qf5 40 Qc8 Kh7 41 Ng3 White wins on the dark squares.

40 Rc1?

Neither player appreciated just how important a unit the pawn at f5 was, and how much the position has transformed by its disappearance. Not only has the g7-bishop now been rendered less effective but, even more significantly, there are now numerous vulnerable squares around the Black king accessible to the White pieces.

Nick de Peyer was right to advocate 40 Rh5! as the best way forward when, after 40...d5 41 Ng5, I was at first inclined to believe that Black holds out with 41...Qg8, e.g. 42 Rf1 Rbd6 43 Qf5 Ba6!.

But here White has a full five pieces exerting great pressure on the Black structure and, after 42 Qc5 instead, Black is in a bad way, e.g. 42..Rbd6 43 Nf3 or 42...Qd8 43 Rf1 Rbd6 44 Qd6! Rd6 45 Nf7, etc.

40...Bb7 41 Qe2?!

Better to have preserved the knight for attack with 41 Ng3, as now he could have gone a long way towards equalising with 41...Be4! 42 Qe4 d5.

41...Qh4? 42 Ng3 Rb4 43 Rh5 Qf4 44 Rf5 Qh4 45 Rcf1 Rd8 46 Rh5?

It was much stronger to have played 46 Rf7!, for then Black cannot satisfactorily defend against the threat of the arrival of my knight at f5 with 46...Bc8 because of the line 47 Rg7! Kg7 48 Rf7 and 49 Qd3, winning.

46...Qg4

My next move is the reason why I chose to include this game. It was not a tactic that had entered my head at any previous juncture, yet it presented itself now.

47 Rf6!? (Diagram 10)

Nunn looked astonished. GM Dmitri Gurevich was later to tell me that he had never seen anything like it from a practical game. For all that, 47 Rf6 should not lead to a win, but it does create the real possibility of an error by confronting the opponent with unexpected complications.

During his 1993 match with Kasparov, Short observed that he was being presented with many problems – far more than those set by any other player. I once heard Nunn, who was also an Oxford mathematics don, lecture that chess is not like maths because the chess player doesn't have to be right – we need only be more right than the opposition, and even then only at the critical junctures.

Chess is a draw if played correctly. Setting the opponent puzzles is one way of greatly increasing the likelihood of his blundering. Perhaps that is one other benefit of an attacking approach to the game.

Anyway, at this point I went to buy an orange juice. When I returned I saw Nunn select...

47...Bf6?

A poor choice of a startled man.

TIP: Attacking play induces mistakes!

The main idea behind my previous move had so intoxicated me that I made only a brief survey of the other lines. The point was that after 47...Qe2? White's remaining forces invade: 48 Rh6 Bh6 49 Rh6 Kg7 50 Nf5 Kf8 51 Rh8 mate. What else is there? 47...d5? allows 48 Qe5, while 47...Rb3? removes the queen's protection.

In fact covering the f5-square with either 47...Rf8! or 47...Bc8! keeps the game well balanced. Finally, there is 47...Kh7, which Nunn cited as his initial reaction. I later discovered a remarkable win with 48 Nf5!! **(Diagram 11)**

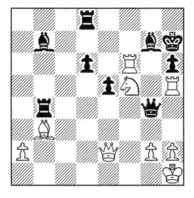

Diagram 11
An amazing position

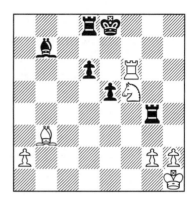

Diagram 12
Technique required

Now 48...Rb3 runs into 49 Rhh6, e.g. 49...Kg8 50 Ne7 mate.

48 Rh6 Kg7 49 Qg4 Rg4 50 Nf5 Kf8 51 Rf6 Ke8 (Diagram 12) 52 Nd6??

After this blunder the game fizzles out to a drawn rook ending. 52 h3!, on the other hand, serves the dual function of rendering the back rank less vulnerable and gaining time through the attack on the rook. After 52...Rg2 (52...Bg2? loses immediately to 53 Kh2) 53 Ba4 Rd7 54 Bd7 Kd7 (54...Kd8 55 Bc6! Bc6 56 Rd6 and wins) 55 Rf7 Ke6 56 Rb7 Ra2 57 Ng3 White will win the ending. By now you might have gathered, when examining this selection of games, that technique was never my strength.

52...Rd6 53 Rd6 Bg2 54 Kg1 Bd5 55 Kf2 Bb3 56 ab3 Rb4 57 Rd3 Ke7 ½-½

The observation of David Bronstein on his game with Oscar Panno from the 1973 Petropolis Interzonal seems to me to be equally applicable in this instance – 'Such a game is played in the air!'

Nunn commented afterwards that when submitting this game to *Informator* I had included hardly any notes at all until the move 47 Rf6!?. But it is quite a move...

This was a scrappy game from a weekend tournament, notable now for the remarkable tactical possibility at move 47. But, in retrospect, we see that the loss of the f5-pawn made the black game critical and White missed several chances to win, notably at moves 40 and 46. Probably, against a weaker opponent, those would have been seized.

The following game won me first place in a GM tournament but is also memorable for another reason – I sacrificed three pieces on the same square!

Game 43
☐ **Plaskett** ■ **Hillarp Persson**
Hampstead 1998

1 e4 c5

The day before this encounter Tiger had blown his chance of a GM norm, something that might have affected his play here. However – to nobody's surprise – he was not long in acquiring the title.

In a game we played at the 2000 Deloitte and Touche Jersey Open he preferred 1...e6, and play went: 2 d4 d5 3 Nd2 Nf6 4 Bd3 c5 5 c3 cd4 6 cd4 de4 7 Ne4 Bb4 8 Nc3 Nc6 9 Nf3 Nd5 10 Bd2 Be7 11 0-0 0-0 12 Re1 Bf6 13 Nd5 ed5 14 Ne5 Qb6. Here I played 15 Bc3, but in the post mortem he drew my attention to 15 Nf7!? (**Diagram 13**)

This possibility had not even entered my thoughts. The point is that after 15...Rf7? 16 Re8 Rf8 17 Bh7! Kh7 18 Rf8 White is winning. Consequently Tiger suggested 15...Nd4!?, when White's knight retreats with 16 Ng5. We concluded that Black's best was then 16...Bf5 17 Bf5 Nf5 17 Qf3 with chances for both sides. However, placing the other minor piece on f5 did not, at first, seem so silly, but after 16...Nf5 there's the chance for my knight to pick off another important defensive pawn with 17 Nh7!? so that if Black takes it White has 18 Bf5 Bf5 19 Qh5 etc.

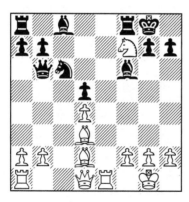

Diagram 13
A strange possibility

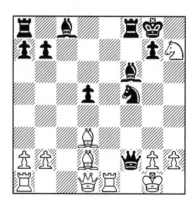

Diagram 14
The queen cannot be taken!

I was pleased with this, and was about to suggest we move on to look at other positions when Tiger halted me and proposed (15...Nd4 16 Ng5 Nf5 17 Nh7) 17...Qf2!! (**Diagram 14**) The justification is 18 Kf2? Bd4 and White must play 19 Be3 because 19 Kf1 Ng3, 19 Ke2 Ng3! 20 hg3 Bg4 and 19 Kf3 Nh4 20 Kg3 Bf2 – or 20 Ke2 Bg4 – are all mate. Black then has 19...Ne3 20 Nf8 Nd1. These are astonishing variations.

The correct response to 17...Qf2!! is 18 Kh1!, with a line such as 18...Kh7 19 Rf1 Qd4 20 Bc3 Qe3 21 Qh5 Kg8 22 Bf5 Bf5 23 Qf5 Qe4 leading to equality.

The right reply to 16...Nf5 is 17 Qf3!, when White is better.

2 Nf3 e6 3 Nc3 a6 4 g3 b5 5 Bg2 Bb7 6 d4 cd4

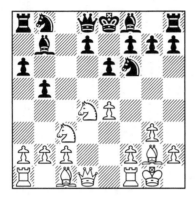

Diagram 15
Black can grab a pawn

Diagram 16
White's knights get working

Eight days later Michael Basman played 6...b4 against me in a London rapidplay. Play continued 7 Na4 Be4 8 Nc5 bc5 9 dc5 Nf6, and I went on to win. By transposition, this position was also reached in a game from the Adams-Short Candidates match in Groningen 1998, when Nigel produced 6...Nf6. That may be the best move (here 6...Bb7) as Michael could think of nothing better in reply than the unconvincing 7 Bg5.

7 Nd4 Nf6 8 0-0!? (Diagram 15) 8...b4

I think that this is a safe enough win of a pawn.

9 Na4 Ne4

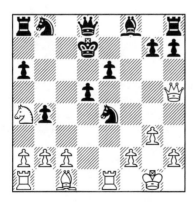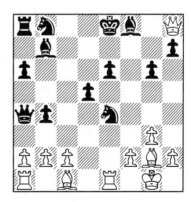

Diagram 17
Black's king is too exposed

Diagram 18
How best to attack?

In a game from the Hastings Open of January 1998, Russian GM Volzhin had preferred 9...Be4 against me. The conclusion was violent: 10 Be4 Ne4 11 Re1 d5 (personally I prefer 11...Nf6 here) (**Diagram 16**) 12 Ne6! (I believe this was an innovation) 12...fe6 13 Qh5 Kd7?? (13...g6 14 Qe5 Qf6! – not 14...Rg8 15 Qe6 – 15 Re4 Qe5 16 Re5 Kf7 is forced) (**Diagram 17**)

The game continued (13...Kd7??) 14 Re4! de4? (this latest offer should be declined as now Black's king is about to be caught – regardless of the extra rook) 15 Bf4 (watch how White's stranded knight now comes into the fray with decisive effect) 15...Kc8 16 Rd1 Nd7 17 Qe2 (as an indication of Black's plight, 17 Nb6!? Qb6 18 Qe8 Qd8 19 Qe6 would also have done the trick) 17...Qa5 18 Qc4 Kd8 19 Qc6 Ra7 20 Nb6 and Black resigned as 20...Qb5 21 Bg5! wins.

Perhaps I should explain that I had just had dinner at my mother-in-law's directly above the venue, Hastings pier, and set out for the game armed with a thermos of coffee which my wife had kindly prepared for me. It was a cold evening and she did not tell me that it had been liberally laced with brandy. By move ten I was feeling decidedly merry, and almost any sacrifice might have appeared plausible. I honestly did not know that my opponent was a Russian GM with a FIDE rating of 2510 and, if I had, something rather more sober would probably have materialised on the board.

10 Re1 d5

In the event of 10...Nd6 11 Bb7 Nb7 12 Qf3 White has obvious compensation.

11 Ne6!

Here we go again!

11...fe6 12 Qh5 g6

After 12...Kd7 I take on e4 with the bishop, when recapture meets with 13 Rd1 etc.

13 Qe5

Regaining the material.

13...Qd7!

13...Rg8? still loses the rook to 14 Qe6, and 13...Qf6? is out of the question as after 14 Re4 Qe5 15 Re5 Kf7 16 Bh3 Bc8 17 Nb6 White wins, e.g. 17...Bd6 18 Re1.

14 Qh8

Not 14 Nb6? Qd6.

14...Qa4 (Diagram 18)

There will be no glory role for the knight this time, but at least Black's queen must leave the action area in order to eliminate it.

15 c4?

This is quite simply a randomiser – and also a poor move. My excuse for this inaccuracy lies in my (this time only metaphorical) intoxication with my previous swashbuckling victory – I threw the kitchen sink at the last guy who grabbed my e-pawn in this line, and look what happened to him!

Tiger said that he had not considered 15 c4. I rejected 15 Qh7 because after 15...Qd7 16 Qg6 Qf7 the attack on f2 forces me to exchange queens. But the right move was 15 f3! Nc5 and now 16 Qh7 Qd7 (16...Qc2 would be asking for trouble in view of 17 Be3)17 Qg6 Qf7 18 Qg4 with clear superiority in material, development and king safety.

15...bc3 16 f3 Nc5 17 Bh3!?

Attacking something soft and important, but again it was better just to take on h7, although this time the consequences of 17...Qd7 18 Qg6 Qd7 are not nearly as clear (19 Qc2!?).

17...Nbd7

Preparing the king's escape.

18 Bg5

Preventing the planned run and therefore rationally motivated, but yet again there was the option of 18 Qh7 when, after 18...0-0-0 19 Qg6, the position is quite unclear and begins to resemble some kind of melted Botvinnik variation of the Semi-Slav.

18...Kf7?

Black defends by introducing the idea of trapping the white queen, but he misses his chance. However, it would require Sadleresque *sangfroid* to play 18...cb2! when, after 19 Qb2 (19 Qh7 threatens mate but 19...Qd4 defends and refutes) 19...Kf7 the attack has evaporated. 19 Rab1 would be a better try here, but now the interpolation of the queenside capture has very much helped Black.

19 Re6

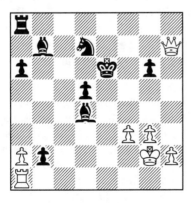

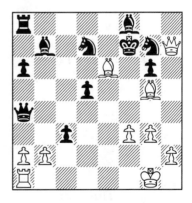

Diagram 19
Rather unclear

Diagram 20
The third offer on e6

Perhaps this is the best move. The alternative was 19 Qh7 Bg7 20
Re6 (not 20 Be6? because 20...Ne6 21 Re6 Qd4! and a subsequent
...Rh8 should decide matters) but I rejected this because I thought it
would lead to a situation where Black had the better chances with my
queen versus his three minor pieces. But maybe not – play should
continue 20...Qd4! 21 Be3 Ne6! (21...Qd3 gives White a fierce attack
after 22 Re7 Ke7 23 Qg7, or even 22 Re1!?) 22 Be6 Ke6 23 Bd4 Bd4 24
Kg2 cb2 **(Diagram 19)**

What is happening here? I imagine White has 25 Qg6, when 25...Bf6
26 Re1 Kd6 might be met with 27 Qf5 in order to eliminate the powerful dark-squared bishop (and thus pick up the b2-pawn). Black also
has 25...Ke7 26 Re1 Kd8!?, so we can conclude that the situation is
wildly obscure.

19...Ne6 20 Qh7

Finally – and absolutely the only move.

20...Ng7 21 Be6 (Diagram 20)

This latest offering is more like a move from Japanese chess, Shogi –
where captured pieces may be used by the opposition and 'dropped' on
to the board – than from our Western form of the game. The bishop
becomes my third piece to succumb to the irresistible allure of the
mystical e6-square as it forces Black's king out into the open.

21...Ke6 22 Qg6

I now wrote down 22...Nf6 on my scoresheet but, with over half an
hour left on his clock, Black preferred...

22...Ke5??

He was three pieces ahead, but king safety is vital in this game, and
he ought to have promptly returned two of them by 22...Nf6 23 Bf6
Kd7 24 Bg7, when I thought things might be pretty unclear.

Here is what happened when I gave this position to the program Mac-
chess 4: 24...Bc5 25 Kg2 cb2 26 Rb1 Bc6 27 Rb2 Re8 28 Qf5 Ke7 29 g4
Qd1 30 f4 Qg1 31 Kh3 Qe3 32 Kh4 a5 33 g5 Kd6 34 Be5 Ke7 35 g6
Qe1 36 Kh5 ... Not that illogical a plan for White; running the king up
the board behind his advancing – yet still sheltering pawns – 36...Qd1
37 Kh6 Rf8 38 Qg5 Ke6 39 g7 and White wins.

That was far from forced.

Jonathan Speelman and Ian Rogers looked at the position after
22...Nf6 during the 1998 Spanish Team Championships, and, instead
of my proposed 23 Bf6, they came up with 23 Re1!?, continuing
23...Kd7 24 Qf7 Kc6 25 Qf6 Kb5. I had quickly rejected this line, as it
seemed unrealistic to think that driving him into the hills would do
anything other than assist the defence. But they spotted 26 Be3!
(Diagram 21) and mate is threatened at b6.

Speelman and Rogers now concocted the fabulous line 26...Bc6 27 b3!
Qa2 28 Qc3 Bb4?? 29 Qd4 Rb8 30 Ra1 Qc2 31 Ra5!! **(Diagram 22)**
and Black gets mated on a4 after 31...Ba5 32 a4 or 31...Ka5 32 Qa1

Kb5 33 Qa4.

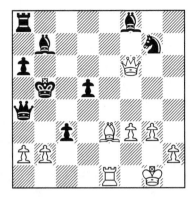

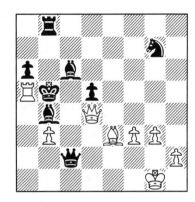

Diagram 21
Black's king still not safe

Diagram 22
A fabulous finish

But Black may also meet 27 b3 with 27...Qa3!?, when perhaps a line like 28 Qd3 Re8 29 Qd3 Ka5 30 Rc1 Ba8 31 Qd4 Re3 32 Qe3 Ne6 is best, and perhaps play is still highly unclear.

I suspect that my 15th move was the pivotal point and that 15 c4? left me unlikely to be able to prove an objective advantage in any subsequent variation. Just several different messes for us to end up in.

Now it ends quickly.

23 Re1 Kd4 24 Be3 Kc4 25 b3

This is what Black had overlooked – I win not his king, but his queen.

25...Qb3 26 ab3 Kb4 27 Qg4 1-0

At his peak, Jonathan Speelman was ranked fifth in the world. By the time this game was played he dismissed himself as a mere 'scribe' but he still has a rather dangerous pen.

WARNING: Attacking play can be a (short) roller-coaster ride.

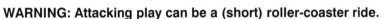

Game 44
□ **Plaskett** ■ **Speelman**
Gibtelecom Masters, Gibraltar 2003

1 e4 d5 2 Nc3!? de4

2....Nf6 is a form of the 'declined' Alekhine's Defence, while 2... d4 is nameless but certainly playable.

3 Ne4 Nc6

3...Qd5!? 4 Nc3 Qa5, as Hodgson once played against me, is a route back to the main lines, but Speelman's move is fine. 3...e5 4 Bc4 Nc5 5 d3 Be7! 6 Nf3 leads us to a restrained type of Italian Game where Black has few problems.

4 Bb5?

This move was sardonically dubbed 'The Gibraltar Variation' in the tournament bulletin by an unimpressed GM Stuart Conquest. 4 Bc4 is better.

4...Qd5! (Diagram 25)

Even at this early stage there is probably no route to equality for White. Note that 4...e5 5 Nf3 f5 6 Ne5 fe4 7 Nc6 transposes to the Schleimann variation of the Spanish!

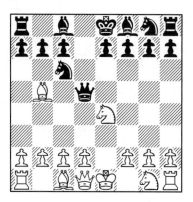

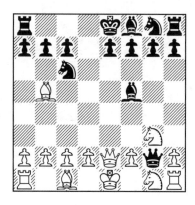

Diagram 25	**Diagram 26**
White worse on move four	Black errs

5 Qe2 Bf5! 6 Ng3

Any better ideas?

6...Qg2? (Diagram 26)

6...Bc2! is the correct pawn grab because after 7 Nf3 0-0-0 Black is clearly much better.

7 Qe5

My counter (I had no alternative), designed to clean out Black's queenside.

7... e6??

Strangely enough, this natural move turns out to be a decisive error! It is now White's queen infiltration that should have proved the more relevant. Black may play 7...Bd7, when 8 Qc7 Qd5 9 c4 Qe5 10 Qe5 Ne5 11 Bd7 Kd7 12 b3 would have led to approximate equality. But best was development with 7... Nh6!, e.g. 8 Qc7 Ng4! 9 Nh3 (not 9 Qb7? Qf2 10 Kd1 Ne3! 11 de3 Bc2 mate) and now 9... Bc8! with a slight advantage to Black.

8 Qc7 Bc5 (Diagram 27)

This is the only consistent move, and the point behind Black's last. I now began to appreciate that my intended 9 Qb7 fails to 9...Bf2 10 Kd1 Bg4 11 N1e2 Be2! 12 Be2 Rb8 13 Qa6 Bg3. Then after 14 Rf1 (with the nasty idea of 15 Bf3) Black has the efficient plug 14....Bf2!, when 15 Rf2 Qf2 16 Qc6 Ke7 17 Qc7 Kf6 still leaves the threat of mate by 18...Qg1 19 Bf1 Qf1 – thus White finds himself material down for insufficient compensation. I sank into despondent thought, from which I emerged only after the best part of an hour...

9 Qf4??

But this is shameless! Psychology is so important in these situations. I stumbled into a position which was already critical at move four. I kept trying, although I assumed that I might already be over the precipice – and quite possibly deserved to be after such careless opening play.

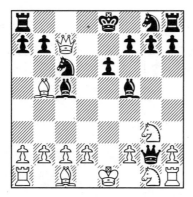

Diagram 27
White has a chance

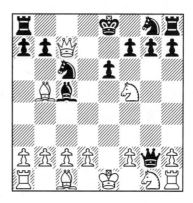

Diagram 28
A computer special

And then there was my track record against Speelman. Between December 1984 and August 1986 I played with Black against him three times. In his opinion, by move twenty in all three games I had a decisive advantage. I lost them all. In 1997 I failed to beat him in a rook ending with two clear extra pawns (see notes to Game 5). The fear factor...

NOTE: Chess is about objectivity.

Later, Speelman (who had first used a computer) informed me that I could have played 9 Nf5!!, a move I do not think either of us had taken seriously. (**Diagram 28**) It looks unfeasible to remove from my king the only active defender, but this is a position of two halves, and it transpires that Black's problems at the other end are the greater. Play might continue 9...Qh1? (9...Qf2? 10 Kd1 and 9...Bf2? 10 Kd1 both win for White; b7 will fall) 10 Kf1! (this cool defence works; the knight on g1 is covered and now it is Black's turn to defend, although there is nothing satisfactory) 10...ef5 11 Qb7 and it's over. Instead there is 10... Kf8 11 Qb7 Rb8, which appears to be the way out until we see the magnificent 12 Qc7!! (**Diagram 29**)

Unfortunately for Black taking the bishop allows mate and even h2 is protected, so Bc6 is a serious threat indeed. Finally, in the event of 10...Nf6 11 Ng3! Qd5 (11...Qh2 12 Bc6 wins for White) 12 Qb7 0-0 13 Qc6 White makes decisive material gains.

Returning to 9 Nf5!!, Black should carry on regardless with 9... Nf6!!, when White must find the correct path in order to keep up the pressure. It is incorrect to go after another piece with 10 Qb7? because after 10...0-0 White will get away with neither 11 Qc6 in view of 11... Bf2 with the idea of 12...Nd5 and a nasty attack (or even the direct 11... Ne4), nor 11 Ne7 Kh8 12 Qc6 Bf2 with the follow-up of 13...Nd5 (or, again, even 12...Ne4). Note here how White's forces are either unplayed or too remote to mount a defence. Of course 11 Bc6?? Qf2 12 Kd1 Qf1 is mate.

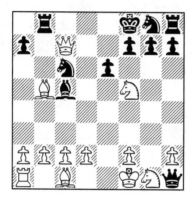

Diagram 29
Wild!

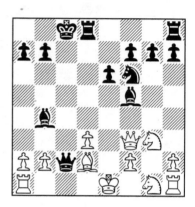

Diagram 30
It could have gone better

The appropriate course is 10 Bc6! bc6 11 Ng7! Kf8 (11...Qg7 12 Qc6 is hopeless) 12 Ne6! fe6 (White wins after both 12... Kg8 13 Qg3 and 12... Ke8 13 Nc5) 13 Qf4! and the queen returns in time to play a crucial role in defence as Black is still unable take the rook, e.g. 13...Qh1 14 Qf6 Kg8 15 Qe6 Kg7 16 Qg4 Kf7 17 Qf3, or 13...Ke7 14 Qf3 Bf2 15 Ke2 Rhg8 16 Qg2 Rg2 17 Nf3 etc.

This all goes to prove yet again the accuracy of Mark Dvoretsky's observation that in complex situations it is not uncommon for everything to hinge on one move, as well as Dr John Nunn's comment after his victory against Adam Kuligowski at the 1983 Wijk aan Zee tournament: 'In complicated positions one must examine every possible move.'

9 Nf5!! does indeed seem to win.

TIP: As the tension mounts consider every possibility.

9... 0-0-0

Black now has a development advantage, the initiative and an attack.

Not surprisingly I did not last much longer.

10 Bc6 Qc6 11 d3 Nf6 12 Qf3 Bb4! 13 Bd2 Qc2! 0-1 (Diagram 30)

Ow! 14 Bb4 Qb2 leaves me splattered. White was winning at move seven... and resigned at move thirteen.

The next game (which decided first place) is rather appropriate given the nature of the sponsoring body.

Game 45
□ **Plaskett** ■ **Large**
Lambeth Arts and Recreation Association (LARA) Open, London 1983

1 b3 e5

Two weeks earlier Peter played 1...d5 against me in a rapidplay tournament and he got a good game before losing.

2 Bb2 Nc6 3 e3 Nf6 4 c4 Be7

One week later Peter played 4...d5 against me in a rapidplay tournament and he got a good game before losing.

5 a3!? 0-0 6 Qc2 Re8 7 d3 a5 8 Nf3 Bf8 9 Be2 d5

Here it is – a reversed Sicilian.

10 cd5 Nd5 11 0-0 (Diagram 31)

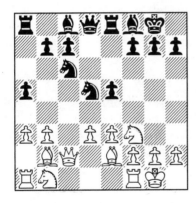

Diagram 31	**Diagram 32**
A reversed Sicilian	Nf5 coming

11...Nb6?!

This is rather vague. An exhibition game from 1970 between Fischer and an adolescent Ulf Andersson continued instead 11...f6 12 Nbd2 Be6 13 Kh1!? Qd7 14 Rg1!? Rad8 15 Ne4 Qf7 16 g4 g6 17 Rg3 Bg7 18 Rag1 Nb6 19 Nc5 Bc8 20 Nh4!? Nd7 21 Ne4 Nf8 (**Diagram 32**) The game continued 22 Nf5! Be6 (22...gf5 23 gf5 is good for White, e.g. 23...Bf5 24 Rg7 Qg7 25 Nf6! and wins) 23 Nc5! Ne7 24 Ng7 Kg7 25 g5 and Black, minus his king's principle defender, soon succumbed.

12 Nbd2 Bf5 (Diagram 33)

A standard Sicilian formation has developed, and one might expect a normal move such as 13 Rac1 here.

13 Ne4 Qe7 14 Kh1!? Rad8 15 Rg1!?

'Ah yes: the Fischer plan' was John Littlewood's remark when I showed him the game, as this had indeed featured in several of Bobby's games. In this case the strategy is made all the more appealing by the location of the bishop on f5.

15...f6 16 g4 Be6 17 g5!

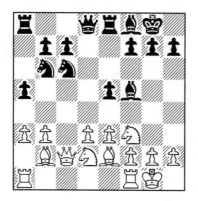

Diagram 33
A standard Sicilian

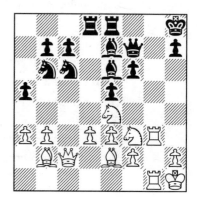

Diagram 34
White has a great attack

White simply marches onward as 17...f5 runs into 18 Nf6! etc.

17...Kh8 18 gf6 gf6 19 Rg3 Qf7 20 Rag1! Be7 (Diagram 34)

In the event of 20...Bb3 I noted that I had 21 Nf6! Bc2 22 Rg8 and mate, but the prosaic 21 Rg8 also wins. After the text Black threatens both to capture on b3 and to neutralise play on the g-file with 21...Rg8. What to do?

21 Ne5!

This sacrifice is certainly the best, but there is one other intriguing possibility to consider in the shape of 21 Qc6 bc6 22 Ne5 (**Diagram 35**)

Black cannot take the knight as 22...fe5 23 Be5 Bf6 24 Bf6 Qf6 25 Nf6 ends the game, which leaves the (forced) retreat 22...Qf8. White can continue with 23 Bh5... what's the story?

a) 23...Bd5? 24 Nf7! (anyway!) 24...Bf7 25 Nf6 and the attack crashes through, e.g. 25...Bg6 26 Nh7 Kh7 27 Bg6 Kh6 28 Rh3 and mates.

b) 23...Nd7 24 Nd7 Bd7 25 Be8 Re8 26 Rf3 and f6 will fall with decisive effect, or 24...Rd7 25 Be8 Rd3 when White has a quaint finale with 26 Nf6! Bf6 27 Bf7! (**Diagram 36**)

Diagram 35
Who needs the queen?

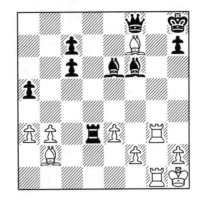

Diagram 36
A fantastic finish

After 27...Qf7 28 Rg8 Qg8 29 Bf6 Qg7 30 Rg7 Black is defenceless.

c) 23...Nd5 24 Rf3 and now:

c1) 24...Bg8 allows 25 Nc6 or 25 Be8 followed by Ng4, both being very strong for White.

c2) 24...c5 25 Ng5! fg5 (25...fe5 26 Rf8 Bf8 27 Be8, or 26...Rf8 27 Ne6) 26 Rf8 Rf8 27 Nf7 Kg8 28 Nh6 mate, or 26...Bf8 27 Nf7 Kg8 28 Rg5 etc.

c3) 24...Qh6 25 Be8 Re8 26 Nc6. White already has a rook and two pawns for the queen, and Black cannot prevent the loss of the f6-pawn (with disastrous consequences).

c4) 24...Rd6 25 Ng5! fe5 (25...fg5 allows the decisive 26 Rf8 and 27 Nf7) 26 Rf8 Rf8 (26...Bf8 27 Be5 and White will win everything back with interest) 27 Be5 Rf6 (27...Nf6 28 Bd6 Bd6 29 Ne6 Nh5 30 Nf8 Bf8 31 Rg5 and White picks up the a-pawn and wins easily) 28 Ne6! Re6 29 Bf7 when Black must move his h-pawn and allow the capture of both rooks.

d) The idea behind 23...c5 is to plant a rook on d4 in some lines and thus prevent White from a kill on the long diagonal. 24 Rf3! is, again, the correct switch of attention for White, with the following possibilities:

d1) 24...Nd5 25 Ng5! transposes to 'c2' (above).

d2) 24...Nd7 25 Nd7 and f6 falls.

d3) 24...Bd5 25 Nf7! Bf7 26 Rf6! Rd4 27 Rf7 Qh6 28 ed4 and wins.

d4) 24...Rd6 25 Ng5! and White wins, with similar variations to 'c4' (above).

e) 23...Ba3. This deals with the immediate threat of 24 Nf7 (24 Nf7? Qf7! 25 Bf7 Bb2) but also removes a vital prop from f6. After the simple 24 Ba1! White's threats return and Black is helpless.

f) 23...Qh6 is a healthy move as Black brings the queen out to play.

f1) White can try 24 Bf7!?, when I believe Black's best is 24...Nd7!
(**Diagram 37**)

Now White should go after material by continuing 25 Nd7 Bd7 26 Rf3! Rg8! 27 Bg8 (I initially thought that a better line existed in 27 Rg8 Rg8 28 Nf6 Bf6 29 Bf6 Rg7 30 Bc3 until I saw 30...Bf5!, which wins because 31 Rf5 loses to 31...Qh3) 27...Rg8 28 Bf6 Bf6 29 Rg8 Kg8 30 Nf6 (**Diagram 38**)

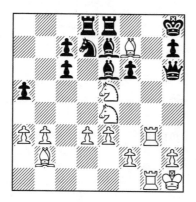

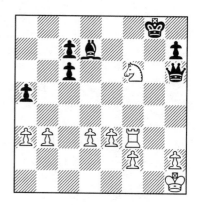

Diagram 37
Black is hanging on

Diagram 38
Can White get organised?

Black may now try 30...Kh8 31 Nd7 Qh5 when White can address the threats to his rook and knight only with the tortuous sequence 32 Rf8 (32 Kg2 Qg4, or 32 Rf4 Qd5) 32...Kg7 33 Rg8! Kf7 (33...Kg8 34 Nf6 forks) 34 e4!, and matters are far from clear, e.g. 34...Qd1 35 Rg1 Qd3? 36 Ne5, or 35...Qf3 36 Rg2. Alternatively there is 30...Kg7 31 Nd7 Qd6. The situation might not seem too bad for White, but he will have great difficulty hanging on to his queenside pawns and this leaves him struggling a little, e.g. 32 Nf8 Qa3 33 Ne6 Kg6.

f2) I also investigated the incredible 24 Be8 Re8 25 Rh3 Qh3 26 Nf6 (**Diagram 39**)

Initially I thought that White was winning here, sample possibilities (amongst others) being 26...Bf6? 27 Nf7 Bf7 28 Bf6 mate, 26...Nd5? 27 Nf7 Bf7 28 Nd5 and mate, 26...Nd7? 27 Nf7 Bf7 28 Nd7 and mate, 26...h6? 27 Nf7 Bf7 28 Nd7 Kh7 29 Rg7 Kh8 30 Rf7 Kg8 31 Rg7 Kh8 32 Re7 Kg8 33 Rg7 Kh8 34 Rg3 and wins and the very nice 26...Ba3? 27 Bd4! Bc5 28 Ba1! and wins (or here 27...c5 28 Bc3! etc.).

However, remember that in complex positions it is necessary to examine *all* moves, and there is a possibility here that enables Black to turn the tables and even win – namely 26...Na4!!, with which Black sets his sights on the most important component in White's attack: the bishop. Play might continue 27 ba4 Rb8! 28 Ba1 Rb1! and Black wins (29 Rb1 Bf6), while 27 Ba1 Ba3! sets up an interposition on b2, 28 ba4 Rb8! maintaining that option. Finally, in reply to 27 Bd4 the only move is 27...Bc5! as 27...c5 fails to 28 Ba1 and 27...Rd8 to 28 Nf7 Bf7 29 Nd5. These finesses will make clearer the significance of 26...Ba3? 27 Bd4!, above.

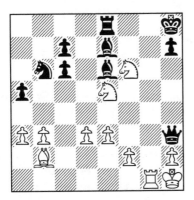

Diagram 39

Black has a brilliant defence

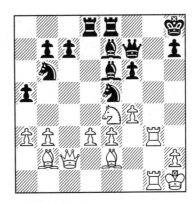

Diagram 40

A ferocious attack

g) 23...Rd6! is the clearest refutation, bolstering f6 and therefore coping with the threat of 24 Nf7. I see nothing satisfactory for White now, and he may have to acquiesce to 24 Nd6 cd6 25 Nc6 with a rook and two pawns and a solid game for the queen, although this could not be fully adequate.

I conclude, therefore, that in the sacrificial line 21 Qc6? bc6 22 Ne5 Qf8 23 Bh5, tremendous though White's pressure against the enemy king is, it is nevertheless insufficient after 23...Rd6!, which means that it is better to keep the queen.

21...Ne5

After 21...fe5 there are no prizes for 22 Qc6.

22 f4 (Diagram 40) 22...Bb3

White's attack is fearsome, e.g. 22...Ng6 23 Ng5 Qg8 24 Bh5 and killer sacrifices are on the horizon.

23 Qc7 Ned7

In reply to 23...Nd5 I planned 24 Qa5 with pressure, while after 23...Nd3 24 Bd3 Rd3 25 Nf6! White succeeds in opening up the long diagonal to the enemy king whilst simultaneously monitoring the one to his own (25...Bd5 26 Nd5).

24 Ng5 Qg8

After 24...Qd5 25 e4 Qc6 White even has 26 Nh7! Qc7 27 Nf6.

25 Qc1 Rc8

25...Rf8 26 Bg4 and Black is under great pressure.

26 Qf1 Rc2

In the case of 26...Bc5 27 Nh7? Qh7 28 Rh3 Black has 28...Re3! 29 Rh7 Kh7 when White's king is vulnerable to ...Bd5. This is another instance of the need to – at all times – bear in mind the importance of the safety of one's own king. Anyway, White has instead the stronger 27 Ne4!, e.g. 27...Qf8 28 Bg4, again with enormous pressure.

27 Nh7!

Decisive.

27...Qh7 28 Rh3 Bg8 29 Qg2

Mate is now unstoppable (29...Bf8 30 Qg8 mate).

29...Bd5 30 Rh7 Kh7 31 e4 Bf8 32 Qg6 Kh8 33 Qh5 Bh6 34 Qh6 mate

Our final game was played in the penultimate round of one of the world's strongest Open tournaments. My opponent was ranked ninth in the world, but perhaps his true halcyon period was already behind him. In 2001 diabetes would end his life at the age of 46, only a few years after its formal diagnosis. In retrospect, I believe that he had carried the condition for a long time before that. He exhibited slug-gishness, especially in the mornings, and his thirst was often so great that during games he would slake it with quarts of milk. These are classic symptoms.

In the last round I would win with Black in 92 moves against Gyula Sax to tie for first with Korchnoi, Short and Gutman. Gutman, inciden-tally, needed only to draw as Black against Simic in the final round to become a Grandmaster. At move16 he declined a draw and went on to win the game, the tournament and his richly deserved title.

Before I won my rook and rook's pawn versus rook ending, the Gods placed this encounter:

Game 46
□ Plaskett ■ Miles
Lugano Open 1986

1 c4 e5 2 e3!?

A novelty – well, at GM level, anyway. Miles had played odd stuff such as this (2 Qc2) himself, with success (e.g. against Sosonko).

2...d6 3 Nc3 g6 4 g3 Bg7 5 Bg2 Ne7 6 d4 0-0 7 Nge2 Nd7

Perhaps at this point we entered new theoretical territory. 7...Nbc6 is known, but given the lack of contact between the two armies in a slow opening, Black can afford to indulge himself.

8 0-0 f5 9 de5

I could not see much happening here so I thought it was worth trying something.

9...de5

9...Ne5 10 f4 might be slightly favourable for White.

10 b3 c6! (Diagram 41)

A classy move with which Black cedes d6 to control d5. However, later in the game access to d6 was to be of considerable significance.

11 Ba3

A killing square to which we will be returning.

11...Qe8

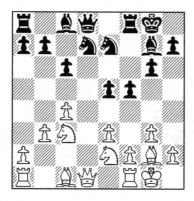

Diagram 41
Keeping White out of d5

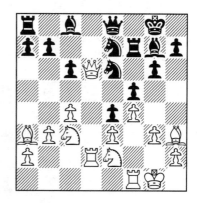

Diagram 42
Not d6 though

11...e4 was also good.

12 f4 e4

12...h6!? is worth investigating.

13 Qd6

One of the longest moves, although it shouldn't really trouble Black.

13...Rf7 14 Rad1 Nf8 15 Rd2

It is difficult to recall what I was thinking at this point.

15...Ne6 16 Bh3 (Diagram 42)

Relocating the bishop threatens to capture on e4 due to the pin on the h3-c8 diagonal. 16 Rdd1 was objectively just as good. Miles responds with the game's first (but by no means last) imaginative move.

16...g5!

Addressing the threat by intending to meet 17 Ne4 with 17...g4! etc.

17 fg5

We have come to quite an important divergence point. In retrospect, 17 Rdd1 was equally sound, for now we find ourselves in a maelstrom.

17...Ng6!

Miles whipped this move out, which – oops! – puts my queen in trouble. But, for some reason, around this time in my life I was feeling as high as a kite, and I strode into the complications like a Macbeth, confident that my charmed life just would not yield to him. And I was right.

18 Bf5 Bf8 (Diagram 43)

White could, and should, now keep his queen, with 19 Bg6 and then moving her to e5, e.g. 19...Rf1 20 Kf1 Qg6 21 Qe5 Ba3 22 Ne4 Be7 23 h4, with three pawns and a real mess for his piece. But I fell for the romantic appeal of a queen sacrifice...

19 Ne4?

For all the riot of emotion and torrent of praise that this was to generate, it is actually a poor move. But the refutation lies hidden deep within the complications.

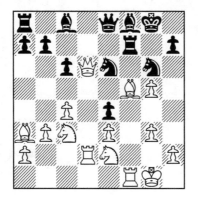

Diagram 43
The queen is in trouble

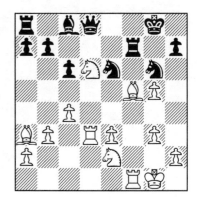

Diagram 44
White plays a quiet move

19...Bd6

Simplest and best. Jacob Murei tried to tell me that this was Black's error and that 19...Ng5 would have refuted my combination. Murei's remarkable mind, as you saw in Game 11, is not wired along any regular scheme, and here he claimed too much. I believe 20 Bg6! refutes the would-be refutation, as the following possibilities help demonstrate.

a) 20...Bd6 21 Bf7.

b) 20...Nh3 21 Kg2.

c) 20...Ne4 21 Bf7 and White wins at least two pawns.

d) 20...hg6 21 Qg6.

e) 20...Rf1 21 Kf1 and now:

e1) 21...hg6 22 Nf6 Kh8 23 Ne8 Bh3 24 Kf2.

e2) 21...Ne4 22 Be8 Bd6 and White wins with either 23 Rd4 or 23 Rd6 Nd6 24 Bc6.

e3) 21...Bd6 22 Be8 (22...Ne4 transposes to e2) 22...Ke1 and White wins after 23...Ba3 24 Ng5, 23...Ne4 24 Rd4 or 23...Nf3 24 Kf2 Nd2 25 Nd6.

e4) 21...Bh3 22 Ke1 and Black has nothing better than transposition, e.g. 22...Ne4 23 Be8, 22...Qe4 23 Be4, 22...Qg6 23 Qg6, 22...hg6 23 Nf6, 22...Bd6 23 Be8 and 22...Nf3 23 Kg2 etc.

One other odd idea which also crossed my mind during the game was 19...Nef4. As with 19...Ng5, I did not overly concern myself with it, reasoning that there just had to be a refutation for such outlandish concepts. In fact 19...Nef4 should also be met with 20 Bg6!, with the following:

a) 20...Bd6 21 Bf7 Qf7 22 Bd6 etc.

b) 20...Nh3 21 Kg2.

c) 20...Ne2 21 Re2 Rf1 22 Kf1 and White will stay two pawns ahead.

d) 20...hg6 21 Qf4! Rf4 22 Rf4 and White has too much material.

e) 20...Ng6 and White may win simply with 21 Nf6 Rf6 22 Qf6.

Lengthy analysis confirms what common sense suggests: that 19...Bd6 was the best move!

20 Nd6

The critical moment.

20...Qd8?

This is certainly very practical. But three other squares were available.

a) On 20...Qd7?? 21 Nd4! is crushing.

b) If 20...Qf8?, there is 21 Nf7 to be considered. After 21...Qa3 (not 21...Qf7? 22 Be6 Qe6 23 Rd8 Kg7 24 Bb2 Ne5 25 Nd4 Qe7 26 Rc8 and wins) 22 Bg6 hg6 23 Nh6. At the time I had thought that this would be devastating, but in the cold light of day it is apparent that 23...Kh8 leaves White with an initiative and a rook and three pawns for his queen – eight points to Black's nine, if you will – but I am still sceptical that he would truly have enough. Despite his slight development lead, he has no direct attacking possibilities and his pawns are split and vulnerable to the circling black queen.

I note that I have 21 Nc8!, as a playable option against 20...Qf8?, when after 21 ...Qc8 (21...Qa3? 22 Be6 wins) 22 Nd4 Black must play 22...Rf5!, and then, following 23 Nf5, he again has a forced reply in 23...Ng5 and the game burns itself out to a perpetual check with 24 Nh6 Kg7 (24...Kh8? 25 Bb2) 25 Nf5 Kg8 26 Nh6, etc.

22...Kh8? would be unwise as after 23 Be6 Rf1 24 Kf1 Qe8 25 Bb2 Ne5 26 Bf5 White has nominal full material equality and Black certainly is not better.

c) However, after the correct 20...Qe7!, the possibility of 21 Nc8 is removed because of a neat refutation which was spotted by neither player; 21...Qg5! 22 Be6 Qe3 and the tables are turned.

Accordingly, White would have to go in for 21 Nf7 Qa3, and there, as I say, I do not think his game really holds together. So that was what he ought to have played.

21 Rd3! (Diagram 44)

Unpinning and so threatening to take the rook. 21 Nf7? Qd2 or 21 Nc8? Qd2 22 Be6 Qe3 or 21 Ne4? Qa5 all lost.

21...Rf5!

After this most practical of decisions Black will have an opportunity to force White to take perpetual check. The only satisfactory alternative was to move the rook away with 21...Rf8! when, again, White will not be able to manufacture more than a draw through perpetual check. It is worth noting that such outcomes are not uncommon in attacking scenarios where lots of material has been invested. Frequently, the player who threw everything into an attack lacks just that scrap of extra time or material necessary to deliver the knockout punch. Here, after (21...Rf8!) 22 Nc8 Qc8 it would be premature to play 23 Bf8 as 23...Ngf8 helps Black consolidate. However, 23 Nd4! is correct, when 23...Re8? loses to the spectacular 24 Ne6 Re6 25 Rd8!! **(Diagram 45)**

This was pointed out by a gleeful Nigel Short after the game. Instead Black has 23...Rf5!, and after 24 Nf5 can address White's projected Nh6 threat with 24...Ng5, when I see no more than a similar repetition to that in the note to Black's 20th move, i.e. 25 Nh6 Kg7 26 Nf5, etc...

Three unplayable 21st moves are:

a) 21...Qg5? 22 Nf7 Kf7 23 Be6 Ke6 24 Nd4 and the queen is lost.

b) 21...Re7? 22 Nc8 Qc8 23 Be7 Ne7 24 Bh3 and the pinned knight on e6 will soon fall.

c) 21...Qa5? 22 b4! with a terrific initiative for White, e.g. 22...Qe5 23 Nf7 Kf7 24 b5! c5 25 Nc3 and Black's chances of survival are slim.

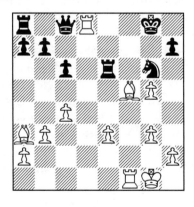

Diagram 45
Nice finish

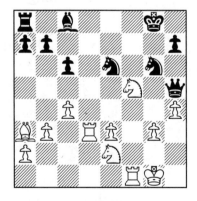

Diagram 46
White has a surprising win

21 Rd3 had three points:

1) To unpin.

2) To protect e3.

3) To meet 21...Qa5? with 22 b4! with a terrific initiative, e.g. 22...Qe5 23

Nf7 Kf7 24 b5! c5 25 Nc3 and black could hardly hope to survive.

That Black can now show no advantage, and indeed should seek to swiftly return material, illustrates the power of white's advanced knight.

Kasparov told me of the view of his mentor, Botvinnik; that to be an authentic World Champion a man must bring something new to chess. As an illustration of a strategic idea he personally had developed, he instructed me that the establishment of a knight on d6 (or d3, for black) when supported by a bishop, may be strong enough to warrant a sacrifice of a pawn, and went on to say that in one of the most classic instances, his immortal win in the 16th game of his 1985 match with Karpov, his black knight at d3 proved to be at least as strong as a white rook.

In the 16th game of the return match the very next year, we were to see Anatoly himself give up a pawn to get a knight to d3, but that one had the back-up not of a bishop but of only a pawn at c4.

In 2000, after Gary's lesson, I succeeded in winning a game as Black against David Howell, primarily through the influence of my knight on d3 supported by a bishop.

Analysis of the position after White's 21st move here shows, in this instance, a knight at d6 supported by a bishop to be so powerful that it justifies the sacrifice of a queen for a bishop and three pawns.

A knight or a giant octopus!? (See my book, *Coincidences*).

22 Nf5!

While Miles was thinking about his previous move I gathered that the text was possible!

Initially I had thought that Black could not now capture on d3 because of 22...Qd3 23 Nh6 Kg7 24 Rf7 Kh8 25 Bb2 etc. But then, to my dismay, I spotted (22...Qd3 23 Nh6) 23...Kh8! 24 Bb2 Ng7, when White has no more than the perpetual check with 25 Nf7.

I was therefore expecting a draw...

22...Qg5?

A very poor decision which may only be explained by Black's having completely overlooked my 24th move, coupled with a great – albeit irrational in this particular case – desire to win. But, as Enoch Powell observed, arrogance is something you *need* if you want to go climbing mountains. Sting considered it one of the most underestimated of qualities, perhaps especially so amongst the reserved English. Miles went very far in chess because of his self belief.

Black now has a lost position.

23 h4 Qh5 (Diagram 46)

The only move.

24 g4!!

Although I say so myself, this is a most unusual winning move.

24...Qg4 25 N2g3 Qh3

This is the only square, otherwise she'll be picked up by something like a check and a knight fork.

26 Nh6 Kg7 27 Nhf5??

A poor move in time pressure. There was a clear win by – logically – bringing the last minor piece into play with 27 Ngf5 Kf6 28 Bb2 Ne5, when White can then choose between 29 Ng3, 29 Ng8 or the prettiest available – 29 e4!! **(Diagram 47)**

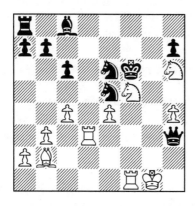

Diagram 47
A pretty win

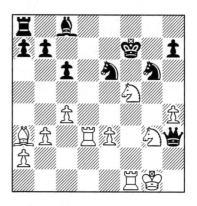

Diagram 48
Black can hang on

Now there comes 29...Qd3 30 Ng4 followed by 31 Ne5 and 32 Nd3.

27...Kf6??

White's inaccurate 27th gave Black a way out – 27...Kg8 would have allowed me to revert to 28 Nh6 Kg7 29 Ngf5 and so on, but Black has 27...Kf7! **(Diagram 48)**

I had assumed that some flurry of checks would despatch him or, if not, then I had 28 Rd2, intending to trap his queen. But matters are not nearly that simple.

a) 28 Rd2 can be met by 28...Nef4! and I see nothing better than 29 Rh2 Bf5 30 Rh3 Bh3 31 Rf2, when I that White is winning.

b) 28 Nh6 Ke8 29 Nh5 threatens mate and forces 29...c5. I do not see a win from here, although White can easily demonstrate a draw with 30 Nf6 Ke7 31 Nfg8 etc. Black may not vary, as 30...Kf8 31 Nh5 Ke8 repeats and 31...Ke7? is mated by 32 Rf7 Ke8 33 Nf6. Note that here the attempt to throw a spanner in the works by throwing a knight on to f4 meets with 32 Rf4! Nf4 33 Bc5 and mate. White might try (28 Nh6 Ke8) 29 Ne4 or 29 Ngf5, but each is met by the shut-out move 29...c5, and there is no win.

c) 28 Ne4 is correctly answered by 28...Ne5!, bringing Black's own knight into the game, e.g. 29 Rdd1 Nf3 30 Kf2 Nh2! 31 Rg1 Kh5 and White does not have quite enough to finish the job after either 32 Nf6 Kh4 or 32 Ng3 Kh4 33 Ndf5 Kg5 (nor with 33 Ngf5 Kh5).

d) 28 Bd6!? (**Diagram 49**)

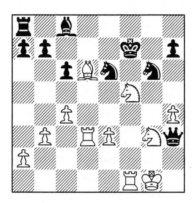

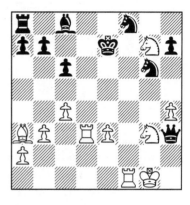

Diagram 49
A quite move

Diagram 50
The king is caught

This was independently proposed by both GM John Nunn and my then girlfriend. Neither gave much supportive analysis. From here the bishop deprives Black's knight the e5-square, playing an important attacking and defensive function. It is not the first move one would consider but, having discovered that the more forcing lines were not winning, it is definitely worthy of scrutiny. Although all of 28...Ke8, 28...Bd7 and 28...h5 could be viable, I shall concentrate on 28...Nef4 because it is the most forcing. Mate is threatened, prompting 29 Bf4 Bf5, Black eliminating a key attacker and hitting the rook on d3. After 30 Nf5 Nf4 31 Rf4 Rg8 Black is certainly no worse, e.g. 32 Ng3 Kg7.

The analysis indicates that after 27...Kf7! Black's development lag and unhappy king afford White full compensation for his material deficit of rook and two pawns for the queen. But this is not enough to win.

By contrast, after the less guarded 27...Kf6?? White might be without a queen but all five of his remaining pieces are ready to throw themselves, like frenzied piranhas, at the black king.

28 Nh5 Ke5

The madcap dash of the king reminds me of Short's 35...Kf5?? of

Game 28, or Hillarp-Persson's 22...Ke5?? in Game 43. Note that 28...Kf7 sees White mate immediately with 29 Nh6 Ke8 30 Nf6.

29 Nfg3!

Locking the door on Black's king and threatening on d6.

29...Nef8 30 Bb2

There were two other mates in four.

30...Ke6 31 Ng7

This is the knight that 24 g4!! liberated.

31...Ke7 32 Ba3 1-0 (Diagram 50)

My opponent's body language indicated that now, for the first time, he appreciated that he was not the one winning this game.

I had been inclined to regard this as the game of my life. But in-depth analysis reveals that he had a much stronger defence in 20...Qe7!, which would have left me at best struggling and, more likely, just lost.

However, I still think of it as the most entertaining game I have played, and find it mysterious how the setting for the alchemy that followed his inferior 20th and 22nd moves, came about.

After the scoresheets were signed we stood up and then found ourselves staring back at the table in silence, drawn by the magnetic appeal of what we had just created, each yet unable to remove his attentions from the crucible.